THE
INFLUENTIAL
ENTREPRENEUR

Position Yourself for Win-Win Engagement

About Kimberly Pitts, UImpact, LLC

Kimberly Pitts is the proud founder of UImpact, LLC. We are a *Branding and Marketing* company, and we are dedicated to helping entrepreneurial women learn and apply branding and marketing strategies to position their businesses in the market, attract their target audiences, create influential brands, realize more income, and enjoy freedom in both their businesses and their lives. We do this through our premier training-based mastermind program-*Thrive Academy*, our *Branding VIP Program*, our *Packaged for Growth Annual Conference*, and a myriad of ongoing training programs.

Anything but conventional, our creative and innovative techniques will challenge you, encourage you, inspire you, and equip you to get to the place you desire, and deserve to be.

Our mission and purpose is to empower and encourage entrepreneurial women to courageously step outside of the box and build towards what they know they are purposed to do. We advocate healthy businesses, healthy relationships, and healthy lives when building sustainable businesses.

Whether you are in the start-up stages of your business or you're ready to grow to the next level of success and expand your reach, we are here to provide expert coaching and mentoring to better position you and your business for greater influence.

If you would like to learn more about us and what we have designed for you, please visit us at UImpact.net.

THE
INFLUENTIAL
ENTREPRENEUR

Position Yourself for Win-Win Engagement

Compiled by Kimberly Pitts

Co-authored by:

Gabrielle Smith
Debbie Saviano
Kimberly Pitts
Alexis M. Scott
Andrea Sullenger
Margo DeGange
Michelle Brown Stephenson
Andrea C. Jones
Crystal Jackson
Judi Snyder

Splendor Publishing
College Station, TX

SPLENDOR PUBLISHING
Published by Splendor Publishing
College Station, TX.

First published printing, June, 2014

Library of Congress Control Number: 2014942749
The Influential Entrepreneur
Position Yourself for Win-Win Engagement
1. Business 2. Internet

ISBN-10:1940278058
ISBN-13: 978-1-940278-05-6
Business/Internet

Printed in the United States of America.

Cover Background: 24613918 Dmytro Denysov | Dreamstime

For more information, or to order bulk copies of this book for events,
seminars, conferences, or training, please contact
SplendorPublishing.com.

Dedication

To the many brilliant and inspired entrepreneurs who have a message, a purpose, and a vision for impacting lives, families, and communities . . . this book is dedicated to you.

"Be around people who have something of value to share with you. Their impact will continue to have a significant influence." -Jim Rohn

Contents

In the Beginning . . .

When I began on this journey of starting my own business, I cannot tell you how scared I was, how unsure I was of whether or not I was working on the right things every day, and how frustrated I became with all the great material out there but not understanding precisely how to apply it.

I literally worked with no real plan or systems in place. The results I reaped were: no consistent income stream, mounting debt, increased frustration, and no real client base. Does any of this sound familiar to you?

You have the passion. You have the drive. You have the desire to accomplish something great. However, things are just not clicking like you expected they would.

My big turning point came one day, when I hit a wall. I personally hit rock bottom. I ran out of money to put into my business. I was getting deeper in debt and that was so scary for me. I felt like a failure. I could not understand why I was doing all the right things but nothing came together.

I ran out of ideas of what to do, and more importantly I was running low on the desire to keep working so hard each day. Here is what my reality was starting to look like:

- I was unhappy and the unhappiness began to flow into my personal life . . . really all areas of my life!

- I was becoming unhealthy with my eating habits (picking up a great deal of weight).

- I stopped doing the things I loved to do (spending time with friends, spa days, movies, etc).

- I threw the most amazing "pity parties" for myself.

I knew something needed to change or shift very soon. I was not given the desire to develop this business for no reason. One day, a good friend came over and held a beautiful, bedazzled mirror in my face and asked me if "this" was who I wanted to be. There is something about looking into your reflection and seeing what you keep trying to avoid. I saw all that I did not want to be anymore.

I did not like who I saw in that mirror. I was aware that change does not happen overnight, but I knew I wanted to break up with the person I saw in the mirror. "She" was not going to help me get out of my situation. I decided to change direction. So I set out to change the course and direction I was going in. I had to ask myself:

- Am I positioning myself in a way that truly represents me and how I want to be known?

- Am I engaging with my target audience in a way that truly connects with them?

- Does my love and expertise of branding and marketing truly influence my market?

I realized I had the right pieces but I was positioning them incorrectly. I was not creating a strong engagement with my audience. I was not truly stepping in and up in the areas in which I knew I could be an influence!

That is what the focus of this book is about. I have met many truly amazing, empowering, and influential women who have had to answer these questions as well. Together, we all want to share with you what we have learned that has worked for us, to help you position, influence, and engage your audience in a way that expands your reach and your business.

Your business is a reflection of who you are: what you value, what your passion is, and what "problem" you wish to solve for someone. How you develop that business will determine how many lives you will touch and change. If you build your business on shaky ground, your business will reflect that.

We don't want that for you!

This book will provide you with the step-by-step processes and give you the level of support you need to grow your business, engage with your client base in a new way, develop effective positioning systems, and more importantly provide you the tools to expand your reach.

Here's To Your Success!

Kimberly Pitts

Chapter 1

The Accidental Entrepreneur
by Gabrielle Smith

I have long referred to myself as an accidental entrepreneur. I can remember years ago helping a dear friend by substituting for one of the speakers from her bureau. As I recall, the original speaker had taken ill and could not travel to the engagement. Since the organization had prepaid for the services, the fees would have had to be refunded; but more important, my friend's reputation could have been blemished because of the short notice of cancellation. Knowing her predicament and how hard she had worked to secure the engagement, I asked if I could help.

I inquired about the speaker's topic. I found I was familiar enough with it to rehearse on the plane (oh, did I mention the engagement was the next morning?), and I fulfilled the engagement. I did a fair enough job that the participants from the national conference invited me to their regional conferences, and those at the regional conferences invited me to their local conferences. And yes, I was paid for each engagement—including the initial one.

What I quickly came to learn is that I did not help my friend out, but rather she helped me. She did not help me become an entrepreneur or a business woman; she did even better in that she helped to launch me into the path of my purpose. What

I once considered to be an accident was actually a divine appointment.

Being an influential entrepreneur and positioning yourself for win-win engagement requires nothing less than discovering your purpose and making it your business to fulfill that purpose—literally!

Influence and the Power to Change

When I think of influence, I think of the power to change without force. Though it is simple in concept, it is an extraordinary feat to foster. It is easy to manipulate and force results, but it is an act of finesse to influence; to affect people, circumstances, and processes for the betterment of all. Influence is a great force and cannot be manufactured overnight. It is far greater than your number of "likes" and Google rankings.

Influence was the most challenging concept for me to accept, though not in the general sense. My challenge was that of *accepting* that *I* had power to bring about change. I know this would be a great place to add a "duh!" and it is okay if you do; just remember, I already told you it is easier said than done.

Entrepreneurship translates to and is often synonymous with influence. As entrepreneurs, we tend to limit our level of influence to marketing and influencing others to take action for our goods and services. We limit our influence to a message or a slogan and hope it strikes our market to action. Now, the point could be adequately argued that this *is* the point of influence and we are seeking to bring about change. Consider this . . . the nature of influence is to possess a power to bring about change without force, however, we tend to indirectly influence and subtly force action. All action does not translate to change, especially when it is done with a sense of powerlessness.

I am not a huge television watcher but one of my favorite shows is *What Not to Wear*. Just from the title you can gather that this is a type of ambush makeover show, but that is only on the surface. The show actually deals with people who believe they are portraying one image—such as *"Oh, I am laid back and comfortable,"* or *"Oh, I'm just not a material girlie-girl"* (a belief in disguise)—while not realizing they are actually portraying what they truly believe, such as *"I don't feel worthy enough to make a fuss over dressing nicely,"* or *"I was considered the smart one of the family and my sister was the pretty one."* By the end of the show, the universal epiphany usually takes on the form of something like, *"I did not want to bring too much attention to myself and make people think (fill in the blank)."*

So what does this have to do with being an influential entrepreneur? Glad you asked. It has everything to do with being an influential entrepreneur. Many entrepreneurs mimic the show's badly dressed contestants who use outdated and ill-fitting garments to fade into the background of their world, while attempting to indirectly force others to believe something they don't truly believe themselves. As entrepreneurs, we attempt to manage the influence of those safe things in our immediate surroundings, but not much more. As a matter of fact, we often equate influence to marketing and nothing more.

Remember, I told you earlier this was the most challenging notion for me at the beginning of my journey. As a first generation college graduate, I entered a world I did not believe was mine. I did not realize I was showing up as a visitor and not a citizen. I was happy and grateful for the opportunities and privileges that were afforded to me, but I did not want to make a big fuss about asking for too much more or believing I could make a big difference. I believed it would be too presumptuous of me to think I had the power to change anything more than the circumstances of my family. I did not want to make too many waves and bring too much attention to myself. I didn't want others to believe I could do something I was not even sure I could—or that I had something I did not possess. My unconscious goal was to stay under the radar.

It was not until I came to learn, know, and understand that the opportunities I was given were more than just those of an education, the privilege of traveling, etc. Rather, they were about access and power, and that power would exceed the needs of my family!

It is said to whom much is given, much is required. I have learned that what's required of me is to not only accept the power afforded me, but to use that power to bring about change. This understanding gave me the authority to do what I have been empowered to do (and it can do the same for you).

Here's What You Can Do

I have three steps you can take today to be an entrepreneur of influence and establish yourself as an authority in your market. They are:

1. Have what you say you have.

2. Do what you say you can do.

3. Show up authentically.

Having what you say you have is much more than having the necessary qualifications. It is more about *not* attempting to be someone you are not. A great part of this lies in owning your power and knowing you have a level of influence exactly where you are. I have learned you get more power by using the power you have! This is not a challenge to get a degree or a certification, but rather a charge to assess what you have to offer, and become confident in *that*.

Consider doing what you say you can do. The operative word here is *doing*! As entrepreneurs we go into seasons of planning, wishing, and hoping and can easily get stuck there. It is only what you *do* that has the ability to influence, and thus bring about change.

Show up authentically in your market to do what you say you can do. Authenticity breeds trust, and trust is the cornerstone of influence. When you foster the first two tenets, authenticity is almost automatic. As entrepreneurs, we often rack our brains trying to create ways to get our market to come to us. How about going to your market? And bring what you have and what's needed! A closet entrepreneur is a broke and non- influential entrepreneur.

Now that you have a sense of how to be an influential entrepreneur, let's focus on positioning.

Positioning is Relative

Previously I made reference to the synonymous relationship between entrepreneur and influence. Here, I will discuss a similar relationship between position and purpose. Merriam-Webster's online dictionary depicts position in three ways:

> 1. The place where someone or something is in relation to other people or things

2. The place where someone or something should be

3. The way someone stands, sits, or lies down

When I was of preschool age I had the esteemed privilege of being raised by my grandmother, Vera, while my parents worked during the day. To this day I have vivid memories of thinking I was simply a smaller version of her. My older brother and first cousin were of school age and attended an elementary school while she and I were at home. It is funny how I never thought I was younger than they were, I simply believed my grandmother and I were the same, and they were the kids.

Now, before your imagination runs wild as to the reasons for my "grown up" persona, let me explain. I remember learning a sense of true autonomy at the age of three; I had "me power." I did not learn I was a kid until grade school because my grandmother never differentiated or varied the value and worth of adults and children. She listened to us, respectfully engaged with us, allowed us to explore and learn, and made learning a part of our daily lifestyle.

I distinctly remember she and I having a daily routine. Shortly after breakfast each morning we began preparing dinner. There was always something that had to slowly simmer to be done at the precise moment my brother and cousin would return home from school. When she shelled peas or green beans, she would put two bowls on the table, one for each us, and divide the peas—my ten to her bushel. We talked as we worked and simply had a grand time. My favorite day was laundry day. I would hand her the clothespins as she hung the clothes on the line. The best part was taking the clothes in and ironing them later that afternoon. I can almost smell the scent of the starch and hear the sizzle of the hot iron as she pressed the cotton shirts and denim jeans. She would allow me to stand in a chair and let my hand rest on hers as she moved the iron up and down the garments; I simply loved it.

One day she and I were taking a break between chores. As we sat on the front porch catching a breeze, she looked at me and said, *"Baby, you're going to be a teacher."* I responded with a chuckle and asked, *"Why?"* She responded by saying, *"Because you are always carrying a piece of paper and a pencil."* We both laughed. She was exactly right because I simply had to have a piece of paper and a pencil every day and I carried the paper around like a sacred blanket. Whenever my grandmother engaged in her daily ritual of word search puzzles, I would sit next to her with my paper and pencil and attempt to scribble something. Thus began my training as a college professor.

Just as my good friend, Kim, launched me onto the path of my purpose, my dear grandmother *positioned* me for my purpose by establishing a sense of self and ability within me well before I understood what that meant. Now, I know what you are thinking, *"Someone with such a strong foundation during her formative years excelled directly to her sweet spot of entrepreneurial success."* I wish I could say you're exactly right, but I would be wrong. It has taken me years of positioning and re-position to discover the sweet spot of my purpose.

Like most entrepreneurs, I spent the time and energy of my initial years in business thinking I would find success and purpose by positioning myself in relationship to the latest trends and well-known trendsetters. My thought was that if I could catch the next best wave of success and ride it to my purpose, all would be well. From flower seeds to income protection (a fancy name for insurance), from Southern style home décor to eye shadows and lip glosses; you name it, I did it. I positioned myself on various paths, just as many of my fellow entrepreneurs did, who "invested" in the promise of fast-tracked success and independence, packaged in the form of coffee, laundry detergent, vitamin supplements, and energy connections. Please know this is in no way, shape, or form a jab at multi-level marketing (MLM); I have been and still am a huge fan and a supporter of such ventures. Let's face it; MLM remains one of the greatest avenues to obtain wealth and financial freedom because the systems work—period.

I would not trade those days and ventures for the world because I met great people, honed my business skills, and more than anything learned what my purpose was *not*. Henry Ford said failure is not failure but the opportunity to begin again intelligently. Well, after many failed attempts at success and being positioned in someone else's market, I realized my success would not be materialized in positioning myself in relationship to others, but rather in relationship to my purpose. I now understand that those attempts were necessary stops on the path of my purpose, because they are no longer distracters to my purpose.

Here's What You Can Do

As an influential entrepreneur, your position must be relative to your purpose and you must find the path of that purpose. The three steps you can take today to position yourself in your market are:

1. Begin where your end began.

2. Let your work be an extension of your purpose.

3. Become known for who and what you are not.

Begin Where Your End Began

Stephen Covey wisely admonishes in his *Seven Habits of Highly Effective People* that we begin with the end in mind and I agree. Based on my experience, I would like to extend his sage advice by saying that influential entrepreneurs who are positioned for win-win engagements begin where their end began. Here's what I mean . . . mentors, coaches, and icons carry the ability to accelerate your path because they possess a treasure map that is covered with dirt, blood, sweat, and tears of *not* having known then what they are now modeling to you. In other words, they make being influential look easy. To this end, choose mentors and coaches based on their journey, not their personality or celebrity.

The cardinal mistake every entrepreneur makes at some point on their journey is they attempt to begin where they want to end. We run out and rent office space before we book our first client or sell our first product. We spend more than we should on marketing material before we have adequately identified our target market, and the gravest of mistakes is that we chain ourselves to the unrealistic expectation of having to know, be, and do everything all at once. We dehumanize ourselves and leave no room for failure, grace, and growth.

If you want to have a talk show with similar influence and effects as *The Oprah Show*, or time-tested quality hair products of Paul Mitchell, or the cutting edge logistics systems of Jeff Bezos and Amazon, you are well within your right and potential to visualize and achieve. Here's the caveat: as you continue to aspire to those similar ends, you must also identify with

Oprah's beginning days of not being a talk show host but rather refining her interviewing skills as a young, inexperienced journalist who endured long days and grueling assignments. You must identify with Paul Mitchell who lived in his car, borrowed money from his mom, and could only afford the now iconic black and white ink to label his products. You must identify with Jeff Bezos as he processed orders on the floor of his garage because he could not afford work tables. To position yourself in your market as an influential entrepreneur, you must begin where your end began.

Work on Purpose

As entrepreneurs we often fall prey to the adage that we have to work as hard for ourselves as we work for others. While this is valid in the general sense, it can also invalidate our efforts. Productivity and effectiveness are not products of busyness; busyness is often a product of uncertainty and fear— uncertainty of what you are doing and fear of its success (no, not its failure). The compulsion to constantly act is often a distraction from this uncertainty and fear. You must adopt the philosophy of working smart and with certainty. You must work within and on purpose, committing only to and doing those things which are aligned with executing your purpose. And though this can keep you busy, you and your efforts will be productive.

Be Known for What You are *Not*

No, this is not a typo! Be known for what you are *not*! At some point in time as an entrepreneur, you accept the reality that there are many people who do what you do or something similar to it. You will also come to realize this is a good thing.

When you don't realize or accept this reality, you easily fall victim to, or become perpetrator of destroying the competition by adopting an attitude of *"since I fear joining you, I will destroy you"* (i.e. gossip, lack of support, undermining, distancing, etc.). This is the wrong position to take. You must become a student of your industry because you are a contributor.

Now with all this in mind, you can become known for what you are not. Simply stated, embrace and celebrate the difference you contribute to the market. Remember, as an influencer you do not force, you own your power to facilitate change by being that change you desire to contribute. Here's an example . . . I recently saw a movie entitled *Baby Mama* starring the dynamic duo of Tina Fey and Amy Poehler. Actor Greg Kinnear played the role of a former lawyer turned socially conscious juice bar owner. The movie was produced in 2008 and the most iconic venture similar to his was Jamba Juice. Each time a new customer would walk in the shop or he would explain his profession, the unanimous question everyone asked with glee was, *"Oh, like Jamba Juice?"* He would cringe and insist, *"No! It is nothing like Jamba Juice!"* Needless to say, by the end of the film he had accepted this aforementioned "epiphany" and began responding by saying, *"Yes, just like Jamba Juice."* The funny thing is, when he surrendered to this truth, people were able to connect to him and were converted to customers.

So, how do you become known for what you are *not*? *"Yes, I am like Jamba Juice **and** I use only locally grown produce from entrepreneurs who engage in environmentally responsible farming practices."* Be the difference you want to make in your market.

Engagement is Active

Engagement is the place where the groundwork of influence and positioning ignite. Engagement involves:

1. Being present at a specified time and place

2. Emotional involvement or commitment

3. The state of being in gear

If there is ever a word which challenges a person to action, it is this one.

Being present is an active process. It requires your conscious attention to each given moment. It is fueled by your consistent assessment of that which is meaningful and relative to your purpose—and this is just the beginning as specificity of timing and location is most critical. Showing up at the appropriate time but in the wrong location could prove unfruitful at best.

I remember having a lunch date with a friend of mine, Dianna. We only get to see each other a few times a year so these luncheons are a treat. We are always so excited to see each other and to catch up on all the events following our last luncheon. We were conscious of the day of the event, and when the specified time arrived, we found ourselves in the right restaurant but in cities forty-five minutes from each other.

Since Dianna and my friendship is such that we value the time we spend together, we quickly decided who would stay in their location and who would travel to the other location. We were both equally willing to travel and equally insistent the other stay at her respective location. This level of emotional involvement—also known as friendship—and commitment, is a decision that is reinforced by our belief in each other and the friendship we share. As soon as I arrived at her location, we burst into laughter, and greeted each other with our usual embrace.

As an influential entrepreneur, your level of emotional involvement and commitment must be a decision you reinforce daily, because it is this level of involvement and commitment that will directly determine your level of engagement and connection.

As a state of being in gear, engagement is the indication of the win-win connection for which influential entrepreneurs are known. This is the element of engagement which affirms your alignment to your purpose and those it is designed to serve. It is this pinnacle to which you rise when what you have to offer is graciously recognized and received by its intended recipient. This is the time and place in which the cycle of change and transformation are not only instituted, but also perpetuated beyond both parties' imaginations. This is the purpose for which you were born.

Here's What You Can Do

My three steps you can take today to engage yourself in your market are:

1. Know your market.

2. Go to your market.

3. Keep the pulse of your market.

Know Your Market

Knowing your market is a notion that is extremely easy to glaze over. Entrepreneurs tend to vacillate from believing *everyone* is their market to believing their market is invisible. Rather than getting into a duel over this matter, here's a simple, two-question litmus test:

> 1. Have you attracted more clients than you can service, and find you have to turn them away or refer them to others in your industry?

> 2. Have your daily, weekly, monthly, and annual profits exceeded your wildest imagination?

Congratulations if you answered "yes" to both of these questions. You know your market so please skip forward. If you answered "*No*" to either question, you must make it your business to identify your market.

Had I known this during my initial years as an entrepreneur, my treasure map would have less blood, sweat, and tear stains. As an influential entrepreneur, you must do the necessary work of matching your purpose and your market if you want authentic engagement.

Consider the following questions:

- Who am I? (This is your story.)

- What do I possess? (These are your qualifications. Resist the temptation to *solely* think certifications and degrees.)

- Who wants what I have? (This is a reference to demographics.)

- Where can I find them? (This is a reference to characteristics and lifestyle.)

Knowing your story clues you in to who you are and what you possess. Knowing your story is an important part of engagement because it cues you to your market magnetism. Throughout this chapter I shared bits and pieces of my life and interests. You had a sneak peek into my sturdy beginning under the wings of my grandmother, Vera. What you did not get to see is how I failed forward through the various stages of my life, and continuously reinvented and developed myself from each fail. My life has given me certain sensitivities and sensibilities which connect me to my market. I particularly work well with men and women who want to develop themselves professionally and experience next-level success holistically.

Go to Your Market

Going to your market is as literal as it is figurative. Years ago it would have been redundant to make such a statement. Many brick and mortar companies began in a briefcase, and many innovative concepts were executed in a garage. Encyclopedias, food storage containers, household products, and cosmetics were sold to customers at their front doors. Now, I am not suggesting you hit the pavement and start knocking on doors; the point I am making is that going to your market is not as far-fetched as you would think. Over the years, as our society and business practices have advanced, this practice of "going to" the customer has changed. Most businesses spend a great part of their budget getting customers to come to them, and there is nothing wrong with this. However, the onus is not solely the customer's. *You* must go to your market.

Today, going to your customer can take on many meanings. Are your customers prevalent on social media? Are they in a particular organization or association? Are they concentrated in a certain area of the community or the country? Are they found on the Fortune 500 list; in universities; in their home taking care of their families? Find out where they are and "go" to them.

Keep Market Pulse

Earlier I admonished you to choose principles over trends and this is a good place to delve deeper into this challenge. Truly knowing your market allows you to learn how they prefer to engage. Technology has advanced to the degree that the means and modes of communication are boundless. The advent of social media and other virtual communication platforms such as Skype and Adobe Connect make engagement possible at any place and at any time.

Although technology has opened the doors to global and instantaneous communication, it cannot replace the time-tested principles of human interaction and marketing. Principles give you the "what" and "why" while trends give you the options to decide "how." Engagement rests on values which require you to learn what your market values and to foster win-win engagement.

You cannot choose your mode of engagement by keeping your finger on the pulse of technology and social media (for it is sure to change). You must keep your finger on the pulse of your market and how they engage to the world around them. Is your market recent college graduates who could benefit from an e-course on building a job-winning portfolio? Is your market soon-to-be retirees who could benefit from an in-house seminar on managing retirement accounts and income protection? The goal is to find the pulse of what your market needs, and use the appropriate technology to meet those needs.

About Gabrielle Smith

Helping others realize their professional potentials and developing leadership abilities has long since colored Gabrielle "Gabbe" Smith's life and career. Gabrielle's training in psychology, and her industry/organization specialization has allowed her to make significant inroads into the local community of the Dallas-Fort Worth area as well as on a national level with motivational speaking and training series through her consulting firm, Visionaires.

Known as the "trainer's trainer" and the "coach's coach," Gabrielle works in particular with organizations as well as with individuals who are experiencing blocks and seemingly insurmountable hurdles, to help them achieve their goals and facilitate change.

Contact Gabrielle at gabbe@visionairesconsultinggroup.com

Learn More Here:
VisionairesConsultingGroup.com

Chapter 2

An Entrepreneurial Journey:
Leadership, Influence, and Digital Leadership
by Debbie Saviano

The world has become incredibly diverse, as has the way individuals choose to make a living. Traditionally, most people chose a job working for someone else with a life of punching the time clock or being under contract . . . bottom line—having a boss! However, there is another segment of society who prefer the road of entrepreneurship, with all of its risks and uncertainty. Yet, with the changes in the economy, more and more people are choosing to select a profession where they are in control. This book is for *those* individuals . . . **the entrepreneurs**!

My entrepreneurial journey did not begin in my early years with lemonade stands, newspaper routes, or dog walking services. Entrepreneurship for me came in my later years, in the form of a second career.

As a child, life evolved around continual moves from one small town to another and going from school to school. My family moved from Texas across most of the western states, as my dad worked in the oil fields.

I was always the "new kid" in class—the child who never knew when she would be moving again; the one who never knew what tomorrow would bring; the child who had to tell herself every day that it was going to be OK. I remember being anxious as to what the next destination would deliver, and yet I also thrived on the excitement of change.

Growing up, we moved so many times I actually quit counting. What I do remember is going to new schools on a regular basis. However, being asked to stand in front of the room and introduce myself enabled me to feel comfortable speaking and expressing my feelings.

Knowing I would not be in any one location for long, I did not waste time. I made friends quickly and I immersed myself fully in whatever activities—clubs, events, studies—that were taking place, as I was eager to soak up all that was available.

So instead of setting up a lemonade stand in my front yard or on the corner, I could usually be found teaching "friends"— pets, dolls, and basically anyone who would sit still long enough for me to be the "teacher." That was my childhood. Teaching and learning were without question the "windows to the world," and I wanted to experience as much as possible. Interestingly enough, I wanted to take others with me on the "journey of discovery."

Attending school in so many towns, cities, and states guaranteed that I would have access to not only a variety of teachers, but teaching styles, curriculum, and various "mores."

Each location had its own traditions, customs, and outlook on life and I was privy to experience them with each new move. Even as a child, I was astute enough to gain a perspective on not only expectations of each society, but I was also able to develop opinions concerning certain basic rights that should be guaranteed for everyone.

Teachers were my role models, and since I had many over the years, each enabled me to embrace not only my love of learning but also my love of leadership development.

I would like to share with you the "building blocks" of my *entrepreneurial journey*. For me personally, there are **three primary areas** I credit to helping me find success as an entrepreneur. They are:

1. Leadership

2. Influence

3. Digital Leadership

Leadership

Let us begin with general *leadership*, and how fundamental it is in regard to influencing others to work with you, to accomplishing a mission, to completing a task, and to all other manners of "getting the job done."

There are **three primary skills** necessary for leadership, and they are listed below along with individual *points of action* for you to consider in regard to your own entrepreneurial excursion.

Leadership Skill #1, Resiliency:

a. Think positive thoughts (meditation, journal writing).

b. Take care of *you* (physically and emotionally).

c. Trust your instincts (listen to the inner voice).

25

d. Establish realistic goals (ones that are achievable).

e. Maintain good relationship with family and friends.

Leadership Skill #2, Adeptness:

a. Develop skills that make you proficient (be willing to share with others the tools that will help them do their job easily and more effectively).

b. Become an expert with certain levels of knowledge (and use this knowledge to make a difference).

Leadership Skill #3, Good Communication:

a. Practice good body language (let the person know you are interested).

b. Make appropriate eye contact (this varies depending on culture, so be aware of what is fitting or suitable).

c. Be present during the conversation.

d. Practice "active listening" (focus on what is being said).

I spent my first career in education as a building principal of five different campuses with grades from Pre-K to high school, and like my childhood years, I enjoyed learning and teaching. So, you see my pathway was traditional in the beginning, in that I knew I wanted to be in education, and unlike those teachers I had admired and respected, I knew from the beginning I wanted to be a school principal!

As I reflect back on it, I am curious as to why I made that decision. I loved teaching and learning, and yet I chose the path of administration.

If I were honest with myself I would say it was because I believed as a principal, I could have more impact with the decisions being made on the campus.

Each experience in life is a lesson for later on and that was indeed the case for the "gypsy lifestyle" of my youth! The ability to be comfortable with *change* enabled me to be flexible and actually enjoy the transformations that life brings.

My entrepreneurial pilgrimage started after I left education, and as they say, "it found me." It was not planned, as there was never time for a business plan, if you will, and it continues to evolve. However, there were many lessons learned along the way and a few qualities which served me well.

Influence

The second building block of my *entrepreneurial journey* is influence. Influence is one of the significant components of a *successful* entrepreneur, and involves five key qualities.

Influence Quality #1, Knowledge:

To be a thriving entrepreneur, having a comprehensive understanding of all facets needed to do business in a particular location, industry, and/or marketplace are integral parts of the equation.

    a. Do the homework!

b. Research what is currently being done.

c. Seek out new experiences, as they help expose you to new situations, people, cultures and lifestyles.

d. Evaluate how it can be done better.

e. Determine what is necessary to begin doing business.

f. Accept that fear is a natural part of the process or experience. When it surfaces, recognize it and make a conscious decision to push through the fear.

Influence Quality #2, Persuasion:

Being able to persuade others is critical for an entrepreneur, as you will need to prevail on others the desire to purchase, engage, believe, and invest as well join a community.

a. Identify how you relate to others.

b. Positive body language and eye contact are necessary for connecting.

c. Practice in the mirror and in front of others to insure the interpersonal skills will draw others in.

d. Don't hesitate to let your passion show. It ignites similar actions in others and people want to follow someone who has an intrinsic desire to do or build something bigger and better.

Influence Quality #3, Determination:

Coming to the decision to be an entrepreneur is one that most of us see as the only option. Being in control of your destiny and being willing to sacrifice the security of a traditional position is determination in full speed. Determination (motivation) is a key for success for entrepreneurs.

a. Set goals along with a timeline for completion.

b. Develop a schedule which adheres to the goals.

c. Structure the day(s) so the most important tasks are completed first.

d. If something doesn't go as planned, regroup, stay focused, evaluate, and start over.

e. Always be on the lookout for opportunities, and imagine how those might be "niches."

Influence Quality #4, Faith:

Deciding to become an entrepreneur is usually something which one has no control over, meaning it is in the DNA and is unavoidable. After all, who would give up the security of a position of working for a stable paycheck in return for the risks associated with entrepreneurship? Yet the answer is fully understood by the person who chooses entrepreneurship— you must have faith!

a. The hours can be crazy.

b. Change is constant.

c. Financial risks are higher.

With all of this, most entrepreneurs will tell you there is no better profession!

Influence Quality #5, Personal Branding:

Your brand distinguishes you above others. One out of three of the world's seven billion people use the Internet. Social media and the Internet make it possible for all information to be easily accessed with a Google search and the click of a key. *Be strategic in your brand!*

a. Colors, logo, design, products, and services are all part of how others evaluate *your* value.

b. It is important to fully understand your core values and belief system so the image you present is an authentic representation.

c. Check all your social media platforms and insure the images are consistent. It is best to have the same professional image on all SM platforms.

d. Insure all of your online engagement is in line with the professional image you desire to project.

Digital Leadership

Being an entrepreneur is one of the most exciting ways to make a living and can be one of the most fulfilling. Entrepreneurs seek to make the world a better place and are willing to take the necessary uncertainties to accomplish this.

Not since the Renaissance in the 1400s has there been such an onslaught of available information. History will reference this period as the "Information Age," a time when the economy was built around information via the Internet.

Thanks to technology, we live in "the land of milk and honey" for entrepreneurs, as there is a direct route to the consumer. Over seven percent of the consumers go online in search of products and services.

With the opportunity to connect directly to the public comes a certain responsibility. In this case, that would be to become a *digital leader,* which is the final area of importance for entrepreneurs.

Digital Leaders are defined as people with new attitudes, new skills, and new knowledge. For the entrepreneur, digital leadership involves recognizing and embracing technology as a means to expand, embrace, and conduct business—all through the advanced use of technology.

People do business with those they trust! It really is that simple. If others have trust in you they will not only do business with you, but they will sing your praises to all they know and become a robust word-of-mouth advertisement.

Social media is the ideal platform to connect, network, and *build* relationships.

Social media encourages and rewards authentic, honest, and transparent interaction. It is the perfect conduit to increase exposure to your business and develop relationships in the process, which is paramount for entrepreneurs. The next time you are dining out, waiting for the elevator, or out in public, notice what everyone around you has in common?

They are holding a *hand held mobile device.* It is through this same device that the public is getting their information. Whether it is about where to eat dinner, meeting friends after work, planning a vacation, or getting directions, it is all being done via the Internet. For the entrepreneur, it is essential to ask:

1. Do you have "signage" on the Internet?

2. Do you engage on social media platforms?

3. Do you have more than enough clients?

4. Are you ready to embrace social media?

Traditional **push** marketing is fast in decline and **pull** marketing is the new front-runner. *Consumers* are choosing whom to do with business with, and they no longer favor the traditional sales model. This is one of the main reasons entrepreneurship is such an attractive model to consider. People are seeking to have business relationships with authentic individuals, and the Internet is the ideal conduit to exhibit that transparency.

Think about it and be honest with yourself; when was the last time you opened up the "Yellow Pages"? Most people admit to taking this unsolicited form of advertisement directly to the recycle bin. The door-to-door sales model of **pushing**— *convincing* the client they need products and services—is diminishing and is even resented by many consumers.

No medium allows for **pull** marketing more than **social media.** With a consistent social media plan, you educate, inform, and interact with the audience (ideal client), all of which are critical to the successful entrepreneur.

Roosevelt coined it best *"No one cares how much you know until they know how much you care."* Social media encourages the development of relationships. When there is a relationship there is commitment and concern.

However, often times when people begin a social media campaign, they transfer their mindset of traditional marketing styles without recognizing it is a totally opposite philosophy.

A solid social media campaign relies on a "***deposits versus withdrawals***" mindset—no "selly selly" and no door-to-door sales.

When you go to the bank, you must have made deposits prior to making a withdrawal. Social media follows the same model.

Following the Pareto Principle, eighty percent of the time should be devoted to making deposits. Social media activity/deposits are the ones which *"ask for nothing in return."* Entrepreneurs should focus on conversations and engagement, and an effective social media campaign should include:

1. Identifying the ideal client and audience

2. Presenting a transparent and authentic image

3. Engaging by being present

4. Presenting information in a non-sales format

5. Building relationships

There is *physical space* and there is *virtual space* for conducting business, and the distinction is becoming less pronounced day by day.

A first impression is just that and we only have the chance to deliver it one time. In the traditional market, most business was conducted in the physical space and the parties had to be together in the same room. Thanks to the advancement of technology, that is no longer the case. The Internet now makes it possible for conference calls, live stream conferences, and virtual meetings to take place without being in the same physical space.

Due to Internet access, business is now conducted on a global scale, and the increase has created an enormous amount of virtual interactions, connections, collaborations, and conversations. As an entrepreneur, there is great value in recognizing the world really is at your fingertips!

Everyone has a *social virtual reputation*; an online image. Positive *or* negative online presence depends upon *how* you and your brand are represented. As an entrepreneur it is imperative that you adopt a positive and active social media campaign.

Are You in Attendance or Are You Absent?

A virtual representation on social media can either be homogeneous—meaning there is a clear and consistent portrayal of *who* you are and the services you provide—or disjointed; confusing and inconsistent.

Social media platforms are viewed as a means of research, reviews, and recommendations, are an active part of the process. Not being present sends a message in itself.

In this last section let's talk about the primary players a **Digital Leader** should incorporate in a social media plan.

(Disclaimer: please know with social media one thing is for sure—it is continually changing.)

Currently, there are **5 Big Social Media Players** (Google, LinkedIn, Facebook, Twitter, and Pinterest), and they each have a solid purpose, following, and benefit. Is your social media platform within the *"Big 5"* current, complete, and active? Does each contain the first impression you wish to convey? Is each representative of you and your brand? Consumers are researching, and what they find will determine how you are viewed. Choosing not to participate categorizes you into a classification which might not be to your liking. Entrepreneurs are expected to be progressive. Incorporating social media into your business is assumed. *Ask Yourself:*

1. Are you on the *Big 5* social media platforms?

2. Is your LinkedIn profile complete and active?

3. Is your online image and message clear and consistent?

4. Are you cognizant of the importance the public puts on social media as a tool/resource?

Each of the **5 Big Social Media Platforms** has its own unique audience and form of communication, and to utilize each one it is important to understand how they differ. Please know *all* social media platforms have one thing in common and that is they are in a continual flux.

For discussion purposes, let's take a closer look at what I refer to as the **"Big 5"**: Google + (Google includes Google + and You Tube), LinkedIn, Facebook, Twitter, and Pinterest).

These are the social media channels where most action is taking place today.

Google +

Google + first hit the scene in 2011 and was designed to improve the way people get their information by combining the features of several of the most popular SM sites. There are "circles" which contain groups of people who are tagged based on designation by you. These include friends, co-workers, and any circle name of choice. Circles were created as an answer to the "personal & professional dilemma." Sometimes you tag someone but they "Do Not Know," only that you have them in "Circles."

Google Hangouts is an additional feature that is gaining in popularity and is basically a "chat" feature.

Google is quickly becoming number two behind Facebook, outpacing Twitter with a thirty-three percent growth in less than a year (*Business Insider*). Estimated global participants number over 500 million with growth continuing.

LinkedIn

LinkedIn is recognized as the ***professional social media platform*** and thus it is imperative you are present. LinkedIn is considered a "**Virtual Rolodex**" and with 300 million (as of April 2014) professionals with an annual income of $100,000+ across all industries, you *must* be in attendance!

If you choose to engage in only one social media platform, LinkedIn is the one to consider. Due to the importance of LinkedIn, the following offers more details.

Professionals *are* on LinkedIn and therefore, it is a given for you to be present as well. However, the representation must be professional and complete. When someone is conducting "research" they will visit both a company (firm page) and the personal profile, and therefore, both must be in alignment with the professional image and message you wish to portray. The consumer wants to do business with individuals, and thus the interest and importance of the personal profile. They will come searching, so be prepared with a strong, professional profile that is one hundred percent complete. For the entrepreneur, this is even more of an asset as they seek to conduct business with you and see you are more approachable and less "establishment."

When creating and designing a LinkedIn profile keep in mind the information must be crafted in a fashion that speaks to the eye! With each word, ask yourself, will this keep the visitor engaged and interested? Does the information convey the image and message you wish to share? Ask yourself, *"Is it an extension of my website—of my belief system and of the passion that drew me to create the business in the first place?"*

As of this writing, LinkedIn does not allow for a choice of font size or font style but there are other options to utilize.

Talk to the "skimming eye," meaning it is necessary to use shorter sentences, bullet points, white space, and use of icons *all* aimed at drawing attention. Take the time to complete the LinkedIn profile and to take advantage of the "space" inside LinkedIn. The "space" equals real estate and is thus valuable. Speak with the same passion and enthusiasm which first drew you to create the business.

Facebook Personal Page

Facebook was the first social media platform and continues to be the most popular. Currently, Facebook boasts over 1.19 billion monthly users and 874 million mobile users and is by far the largest SM network. However, in recent months Facebook has been losing traction especially in the business sector. "Facebook *is* the Social Platform" (*Entrepreneur Magazine*). From a psychological standpoint, it is very difficult to move from a social mindset into a professional, business one. Therefore, most would argue that trying to conduct business on Facebook is a challenge. The latest adjustment of moving the ADS into the main feed is a means to garner more interest and it seems to be working. The biggest conversation around Facebook is the *personal versus the professional conversation.* As mentioned earlier, many people believe it is possible to separate the two and I would argue it is not a solid reality.

Take a look at the number of cameras that are present "everywhere." Privacy is defined much differently today than in the past, and as technology improves we move closer to the reality that there is *no privacy in the public sector.* Remember all those hand-held devices? They all have cameras and no longer do people ask for permission before snapping a picture. I also contend that as an entrepreneur, you have an advantage if you are transparent enough to be willing to open yourself up via your personal Facebook page.

Twitter

Most individuals have a like/dislike relationship with Twitter and I would say it is due in large part to the user's learning style. Twitter is noisy, chaotic, constant chatter, and some love it while others are easily irritated by it. However, the question that arises is, "*Do your clients and target audience like and use Twitter?*" After all, that is the question, as it is about *them!*

Twitter is credited with the on-the-ground coverage of the Egyptian Revolution, and some go as far as to say it helped in the organization of the revolution (*Wired*). With monthly users of 232 million, Twitter is popular, and recently underwent changes on the *Profile View* (April 2013). Depending upon your own learning style and preference of how information is received, Twitter is a contender, and with over 200 million users, well worth considering as part of any social media campaign.

Pinterest

All one has to do is say "*Pinterest*," and for those who are familiar, the "sighs and smiles" emerge. Pinterest is a visual social media platform with more than seventy million addicted users. Images increase learning, and therein lies the value of Pinterest. Images are emotional connectors, and as a visual platform, Pinterest is queen, and this is supported by the fact that it dominates referral traffic (*Forbes*).

Pinterest is similar to a large bulletin board separated by individual mini-boards. Businesses have been slow to recognize the significance of Pinterest, but that is quickly changing. Businesses are beginning to take advantage of a very loyal customer base inside Pinterest and are, as they say, "joining the party."

So, we have covered all of the **Big 5 Social Media Platforms**, and shared some high points on each. Hopefully by this point, there is interest in either beginning the journey or in stepping up on what is already taking place. If you want to be regarded as an expert in your field, and you want to connect directly with your target audience, social media is ideal! Present yourself as a ***Digital Leader*** for the purpose of communicating directly with those who are in need of your services, either today or tomorrow.

In Conclusion, are You a Digital Leader?

✓ Do you value social media as a marketing tool?

✓ Are you using social media to attract the clients who are in need of your services?

✓ Is your social media image and message clear and consistent?

✓ Is your social media communicating directly with clients and potential clients?

✓ Have you converted from the mindset of *push* to the mindset of *pull* marketing?

✓ Do you have a social media campaign designed to communicate, educate, engage, and serve?

Hopefully, by now you are *ready*, *willing*, and *able* to embrace social media as a means to serve your clients and the marketplace. Keep in mind that regardless of where you are in the ***Entrepreneurial Journey***, consider **Leadership, Influence, and Digital Leadership** as the fundamental basis to assist you. I am wishing you continued success as an entrepreneur!

About Debbie Saviano

Debbie Saviano spends her time helping other professionals *"Take action and create an online presence"* by developing, nurturing, and maintaining relationships!

With a background in education and a degree in English, History, and Psychology, Debbie implements a practical approach to social media.

Speaking and training enable Debbie to remain close to those interested in continuing to learn and embrace technology as well as innovative methods to build relationships.

Debbie started her first career driving a yellow school bus and retired after being a principal of five campuses. Today, Debbie navigates the "virtual highways" and in doing so shows others how to connect, engage, and relate to those they can serve.

Learn More Here:
DebbieSaviano.com

Continue the Conversation on . . .

Facebook: Facebook.com/debbie.saviano
Twitter: Twitter.com/debbiesaviano
Pinterest: Pinterest.com/debbiesaviano
LinkedIn: Linkedin.com/in/debbiesaviano

Chapter 3

Position Your Brand for Impact and Engagement
by Kimberly Pitts

The Tiffany's blue box was first introduced in 1837. The color known as Tiffany Blue was selected by founder Charles Lewis Tiffany for the cover of *Blue Book*, Tiffany's annual collection of beautifully handcrafted jewels, first published in 1845. Tiffany Blue is also referred to as Robin's-Egg Blue or Forget-Me-Not Blue. This distinguishing color may have been chosen because of the popularity of the turquoise gemstone in 19th-century jewelry. This one blue box represents high value, great quality, and luxury. When someone receives this blue box they instantly feel valued by the one giving it.

It is amazing that Charles Lewis Tiffany realized early on the importance of brand positioning at a time when few people thought about such things. He determined that the color blue would be associated with Tiffany & Co and introduced the box, knowing he could differentiate gifts from his store that were presented in the distinctive box. Tiffany's classic Pantone No. 187, the color code for the blue box, demonstrates that a brand can maintain its relevance in a competitive market for more than 150 years by being consistent in its brand attributes and associations. Tiffany retains and maintains a differentiation strategy of highly perceived value. The incremental costs of their jewelry might not be that much higher than competitors, but the perceived worth to customers is much higher and they are willing to pay more to get a Tiffany item.

To this day, the blue box is one of the most coveted and most protected brand attributes of Tiffany & Co. Without the box, the value of the contents reduces instantly. With the box, it becomes a true piece of differentiated luxury. The brand has been positioned so strongly in the market that people focus on the perceived value of Tiffany versus the actual value of the jewelry the box contains.

So how does Tiffany's brand positioning apply to you? Glad you asked! Before I jump in and share with you how the Tiffany & Co blue box example applies to you, let me ask you a question. Do you presently have a business brand that clearly expresses who you are, who you work with best (those amazing people you love to serve), what your values are, and what benefits you deliver, and does your brand attract clients on a consistent basis? If your first response is, "*Yes, I have a brand that does that,*" then I say "*Congratulations!*" If your answer is, "*I think I have a brand that does that,*"or "*No, I don't have a business brand that consistently attracts my ideal clients,*" then I encourage you to read on. An effective brand allows people to get to know who you are and it positions the core of your business. It creates a personal, responsive (emotional) connection to you. Understanding and formulating your brand is the foundation and the heart of your business. Before marketing . . . before networking . . . before jumping out there (or restarting) . . . branding should be at the core.

To really gain the value of what it means to position your business brand in a way that differentiates you and aligns you with your audience, I want to impress upon you to a make a list of all the entry points into your business. This may include your blog, website, social media platforms, joint venture relationships, teleseminars, webinars, books, CDs, DVDs and the list can go on. Look at what you are communicating and how you are building your brand. Creating a relatable and breathable brand that feels totally on point for your vision for your business is vital to building a sustainable and profitable business. You need to be crystal clear on how to articulate your messaging to your clients, team, and prospective clients on the front lines. What do you feel you need to do at this point to build an influential brand?

The Tiffany & Co example illustrates the strength of designing a brand value and position that allows you to consistently stand out in the market place and in the minds of your target audience. That is why I wanted to include their example when discussing the importance of positioning. You chose to read this book because you want to strengthen your brand positioning, elevate your level of engagements, and amplify your level of influence. So I want to go ahead and jump in and share with you some key insights on how you can start positioning yourself.

Those embracing classical marketing will recognize position as one of the 4Ps (Position, Price, Place, and Promotion). There's a lot we can say about position; how to measure it, how to change it, etc., but for the purpose of getting a good start with your inbound marketing, the two concepts you need to understand and track are position and positioning. There's a difference. It's imperative. And it's often confused.

Position is the way your prospects view your business. Your prospects position you. You do not position yourself. One of our clients has a position in the market for executive leadership development. Those who have attended her invitation-only trainings create that position. That is the way they see her brand. There is nothing she can do about it.

Knowing your position, you may want to be someplace other than where you are. That's positioning. Most small business owners for example, have goals for their market position. They have positioning goals. Their positioning statement defines those goals, and the goals support their objectives.

When you think about companies like Tiffany & Co., Nike, and Dove, you are immediately connected to their brand image. Their image is imprinted on how you think about their services, products, offerings, and advertisements.

- Nike prompts you to think about all things sports and Michael Jordan.

- Dove prompts you to recall the commercial with women from all walks of life sharing how beautiful they are regardless of race or physical size.

- Tiffany prompts you to think about luxury and romance.

Now I want you to ask yourself some questions. What do you want people to think of when they think, feel, and connect to what you do? Keep in mind it is all about connection, being true to yourself, and being meaningful so people take notice and care, and it must be powerful enough to make the difference you desire.

- Do all elements of our branding strategy integrate with one another?

- Are these elements delivered consistently?

- What problem are we attempting to solve?

- Has there been a change in our industry landscape that is impacting our growth potential?

- Has our customer profile changed? (This is a great question to ask yourself each year you're in business.)

- Are we pigeonholed as something we (and our clients and customers) have outgrown?

- Does our brand tell the wrong (or outdated) story?

- What do we want to convey? To whom?

- Why should anyone care about our brand?

- Will this solution work five, ten, and fifteen years from now based on what we can anticipate?

- Have we isolated *exactly* who should care about our brand?

- Have their needs—*or the way they define them*—changed?

- Are we asking our customer to care more about our brand—and what it means—than we do?

- Is our brand associated with something that is no longer meaningful?

- Is our brand out of step with the current needs and desires of our customers?

- Are we leading with our brand direction?

- Are we following with our brand direction?

- Is the goal of our brand positioning strategy a stepping stone (evolutionary), or a milestone (revolutionary)?

Review all the questions listed and really take some time to examine how your responses are impacting your business today. This is the process I took many years ago. When I first entered into the coaching industry, I was clueless as to how to make myself stand out, let alone how to position myself as an authority in the marketing and branding space. I used to consistently undervalue myself and over-deliver, and I had no real boundaries with my clients. They contacted me day and night, as I had an open door policy. I wanted to be "that" coach that was always available to their clients. I had used that as a selling point. It is funny to me now that I really thought I was positioning myself in a strategic way. However, I had actually opened the door to burnout, frustration, and stress. So, I knew that approach would not work.

This is the approach I see so many of you take. You know personally you have a lot to offer others, but that is not being communicated in your marketing materials, in the entry points to your business, or in the programs and services you offer. If your value is not being communicated, it is hard for clients to know how to value what you offer.

When I launched my business many years ago, I found myself wondering how I could really stand out and grow my business. There were many people offering what I was offering in the field of coaching/mentoring, especially in the areas of marketing and branding. However, I knew I did not believe in competition and I knew there was plenty of business for everyone. Yet, I needed to dig deep and discover what value I offered someone.

I quickly grew to realize that what I have to offer is unique to me. I can't be like anyone else because I have not walked in their shoes nor have I gone through their ups and downs that got them to where they are today. So one evening, I decided to write out all the end results my clients walked away with when working with me. I based this on what was shared with me by my clients. As I kept writing and reviewing my clients testimonials, my value list really emerged. This exercise changed how I communicated what my business brand offered to potential and existing clients.

What I did next was review all the entry points into my business to see if I was being consistent in communicating my value, the vision of my company, and the purpose of why I started UImpact. When I checked my website, blog, and social media outlets, I saw I was not communicating any real value at all. I spoke more to the *features* of what I offer and not the benefits. That was a huge mistake! You will find that by not communicating your value to your clients, you will be constantly trying to convince people to work with you. So let's jump into this next exercise.

Values

Make a list of twenty ways you bring value to your clients. This list can include the benefits your clients have shared they've received from you. (Ask yourself which entry points show your value the most and the least.)

Color

The most prominent and influential brands in the world are defined by their colors. Consider Target's red bullseye image and UPS' slogan, *"What can brown do for you?"* These companies, and many others, strategically use colors in their logo, website, and product to appeal to customers. As a business owner/entrepreneur, it's imperative to think about how you utilize colors and what the colors you choose say about your business.

Research has found that different colors provoke very different reactions in people. Integrating your brand colors into your logo, landing pages, products, and more will help you achieve the highest impact. Conduct a quick survey of your current audience and those you trust, and ask them what they feel the color choices you have selected, communicates to them. Do your brand colors engage them, make them excited, repel them, make them think of something positive or negative, etc?

Before you start marketing, branding, or networking, you must look at yourself and your business and determine your *KLT Factor*. The KLT Factor is the **Know-Like-Trust** Factor. This positioning-based and relationship-building approach in business is growing exponentially because it works to consistently build loyalty, sales, and a solid platform for all future product or service launches. Mastering these three areas will position you greatly in front of your audience.

Customers or clients must have a connection to you on all three levels before they purchase from you and become long-term buyers. You can be in front of prospects for many months before they purchase from you. Experts say seven or more impressions are required before people feel they know, like, and trust you enough to give you their money. I know that does not sound great, however look at it as a fun challenge. Brainstorm all the various ways to be in front of your audience on a consistent basis.

Think about it; it makes sense. The evolution of any relationship takes time to establish and maintain. It may seem odd at first to transfer personal relationship concepts to business connections, but it's not. Genuine connection to each other is an essential component in any relationship. When we conduct business as an extension of our personal lives and philosophies, it's a no-brainer. It is simply good business to establish a method by which prospects can get to know, like, and trust you as a proven, strategic method of achieving results.

Let's break down each area in more detail. It is very important to me that you really grasp how to apply these principles to your business.

Know

You want to help your target audience and current clients get to know you. You want them to say things such as, *"I've heard of (or seen) your name. I've seen you around, I've heard about you and/or your company, and I think I know something about you."* They may or may not know much but they have a sense they do.

So how do they get to know you? Through how you present your business brand; through your speaking engagements, blogs, newsletters, client testimonials, social media, and from any published materials you have.

Like

"Know" alone is not enough. It is helpful, but if you want people to consider buying from you then you have to build a bridge to trust and like. People may know all about you, but you still have to make that personal connection. You want them to say, "*I like your style. You make me feel comfortable and I get a sense you care about me.*" "Like" reflects how people connect with you. While it is great that they enjoy your content and information, they need to cross over and like the person behind the brand.

Let's look at an example of this. I remember having the opportunity of meeting one of my favorite authors. I truly loved everything she wrote and the imagery she always displayed in her writing. When I learned she was hosting a book signing in my city, I was so excited to meet her. (She had positioned her business brand to create a raving fan: me!) When I attended the book signing and had the opportunity to meet her, my excitement quickly waned. She was very unfriendly, unapproachable, and unapologetic for how she was treating us . . . those who loved her product. Since that evening a few years ago I have not bought anything else from her. Her likeability was tarnished for me.

You see, when positioning your brand, it is vital to help your audience get to know you, but you must create a connection so they will like what you have to offer. So how does this show up in your business? Your regular attendance at networking events can launch the "like" factor. Standing in your authentic self in every situation is vital. You can create a video that showcases your expertise.

Trust

People may feel like they "know" you and they can even "like" you, but if they don't trust you to deliver a service that positively impacts their lives—or business—you may not gain a new client. Trust is rooted in delivering genuine information and content. It is rooted in showing you care about your clients and potential clients. Trust is also rooted in how you share your level of expertise. You want them to say things such as, *"Not only do I like you but I feel you have enough expertise in solving my problem that I'm willing to pay you good money to do that. It will be worth the return on my investment."*

Take a minute and think about the brands and people you are most connected to. How do those brands/people make you feel? Do you trust what they are offering? Do you trust you will get what you paid for? Additionally, think about why you bought from that brand or supported that person. If you ask yourself if you know what they stand for, like what they had to offer, and trust the result you would get, you will see how the KLT Factor works in developing connections and relationships with potential and actual clients. By developing these connections, you position your business brand in a distinctive way of standing out.

We are going to switch gears now. We have been talking quite a bit about positioning your business brand. What I would like to do now is share why it is equally vital to position your personal brand as well. Since the majority of the audience reading this book will be solopreneurs and small business owners, your personal brand is equally important to building a successful business.

What do Sir Richard Branson, Barack Obama, and Suze Orman all have in common? They have each built powerful personal brands that have propelled them to the top of their businesses, their careers, and their lives. How did they do it? Like other successful personal branders, they took the time to define, communicate, and protect their brands. You can be sure they followed each of the **top ten insights** below to reach their great success. There's no magic to it: you can apply the same personal branding principles to your work and life, not only to achieve your goals, but to *surpass* them.

You see, many marketers have misunderstood the term "brand." People will talk to you about your logo, website, stationary, and elements along those lines as your brand. However, that is not your brand. They are components that help to build your business and they assist in identifying you to your target audience. Your brand is based on how you are perceived, what you project, and how your target perceives the value you have to offer.

Insight #1

You already have a personal brand whether you want one or not—simply by virtue of being you, either as an entrepreneur or in the workplace. It's up to you to determine where your personal brand is strong and where it could use improvement. Then, it's up to you to make the changes necessary to make it as strong as possible.

Insight #2

Your personal brand exists in the minds of others in the way they *perceive, think, and feel* about you. Think about your favorite corporate brand for a moment. It can be the best "functioning" product of its kind in the world, but if the public fails to *perceive* it as the best, it won't be successful. So, it's critical to keep in mind that your personal brand is not what *you* think it is but it's what *others* perceive it to be.

Insight #3

A common misconception about personal branding is that it's self-centered and all about *you*. But the truth is, personal branding is all about your target audience—the person or people you most want to impact with your brand within your target market.

Just as corporate branders must offer a benefit to consumers in order for a product to be a success, you must fill a need with your target audience with your products and services. That is why it is so important to make sure you understand the needs and wants of the audience you are targeting.

Insight #4

Since your personal brand exists in the minds of your clients and customers, the only way to determine if your brand is successful is to find out how your customers and clients perceive you. If there is a gap between what your customers and clients think and feel about you, and what you *want* them to think and feel about you, your personal brand should be adjusted and strengthened. You can do this through surveys, focus groups, or simply sending them an email asking for the feedback.

Insight #5

The only way to have a strong personal brand is to carefully *define* it. Many people believe personal branding is all about how you "execute" your brand, but true personal branding starts with a crystal clear definition of what you would like to be known for. Until you define it, your brand is just a vague premise with no real foundation. No successful entrepreneur would dream of putting a product in the marketplace without a clear definition of the brand.

That definition tells the entrepreneur which consumers to target and where to focus their client attraction strategies. On a personal level, your own brand should do the same.

Insight #6

The best brands respond to both *emotional* and *functional* needs. In your business, functional needs are the tasks you perform on a day-to-day basis. The emotional needs you fill forge a very important connection with your target market. Remember, your target audience looks at what needs you fill for them whether personal or professional.

Insight #7

The best personal brands are credible, so you must *prove* you can deliver what you promise. It isn't enough simply to *say* you can fill a need at work; you must *show* you have the experience and/or training to do it. People do business with those they feel they know, like and trust. Your personal brand should be rooted in being authentic and full of integrity.

Insight #8

Your personal brand is built 24/7 and 365 days a year through what you say, but even more importantly, through what you *do*. This doesn't mean you can't be human or make mistakes, but it means that you need to think about behaviors that could damage your brand, such as how you talk to a customer who has angered you, how you respond to negative feedback, and how you handle a customer when your day has been difficult.

Insight #9

While it's important to avoid negative behaviors that can undermine your brand, it's also important to be *consistent* in how you communicate your brand. If Nike's ads suddenly focused on encouraging you to become a couch potato, you wouldn't know what to think, would you? Just as Nike is consistent in promoting sports and fitness in all of its advertising, you must be consistent in how you present your personal brand every day. If you *occasionally* make a blog post, *sometimes* respond to an email, or update your website every *other* week, those actions tell your customer how you think and feel about them. Consistency builds trust. It builds credibility and it builds reliability.

Insight #10

Even though your personal brand is all about your target market, it never makes sense to pretend to be someone you are not. People can generally tell when you are not being authentic and when you are not conducting your business in a spirit of integrity . . . meaning you are not being who you really are.

So, the task is to find out what your target market needs, then align those needs with your own *unique strengths* and your unique *character* traits. Your personal brand will then reflect who you really are, which will not only bring you greater success in your business, but greater fulfillment as well.

You don't have to be famous to benefit from defining, communicating, and protecting your personal brand. But you can certainly learn from their examples and take advantage of the same personal branding secrets that have helped the heavy hitters reach their full potential.

Now that you have a great understanding about positioning, I wanted to share some insight on how effective positioning affects buying decisions. Believe it or not, no one actually buys your service. No one buys coaching. No one buys consulting. No one buys financial planning. So what do people buy? Well, there are, in fact, two things people buy.

People Buy Solutions

The first thing people buy is a solution to a problem. People buy a service only because they believe it will solve certain problems and give them certain results. They do not buy the "how" of a service. Your service is simply the tool or method you use to solve problems and deliver results (the "*how*" you do it).

Do you buy a hammer because you just want a hammer? Do you buy a car because you just want a car? Do you go to the dentist because you happen to feel like being drilled? These examples show you are buying a solution to a problem; you are buying a result. You would not buy a hammer, a car, or go to the dentist unless they all solved problems and delivered results.

Just suppose you focus on telling someone all about "how" your coaching and consulting service works and what it is. At the end of the conversation (if they are still listening), they will have a good understanding of your "how" but they'll be left wondering what problems you will solve for them and what results you will deliver.

If people do not know what problems you will solve for them and the results you will deliver, it is highly unlikely they will buy your service. If however you focus on understanding their problems and the results they will get, you will be focusing on what people are buying and your chances of success will be dramatically increased.

People Buy YOU!

The second thing people buy is *you*! Once someone has decided they have a problem they want solved, they make a decision as to who will solve it for them. If you have focused the conversation on telling them all about your "how" and what your service is, they will feel you are focused on yourself and your needs. When the focus is on you, people get the sense that you have your own best interests at heart and you don't really care about them. They will start to think you are simply trying to sell them something, and all sorts of sales resistance will surface.

If you've been focusing the conversation on understanding their problems, they will feel you have their best interests at heart. They will start to trust you and open up to you. They will naturally decide you are the person to solve their problems (assuming of course there are problems to be solved, etc).

In summary, don't focus on selling your services. Instead, have conversations where you focus is on understanding problems, and then people will assume you know "how" to deliver results. The more you focus on understanding their problems, the more they will trust you are the one they should be working with. That is how positioning affects the buying decisions of your target audience.

Actionable Items

The following give an overview of questions you can ask yourself to evaluate whether or not you have consistent brand messaging. While we addressed some of these questions above, I want to encourage you to sit down and spend some time considering and answering these questions. The clearer you can be in answering each one, the clearer your content, position, and positioning will be.

Brand Evlauation Questions:

- Is your brand associated with something that is no longer meaningful?

- When you look at all of the entry points into your business, is your brand message consistent and clear?

- Does your brand create an emotional connection with your audience? Does it compel them to want to get to know you . . . or stay connected to you?

- Are you clear on what your brand is and the message you want to convey?

- Are the attributes of your brand clear throughout your business?

- Are you attracting the clients, partners, joint venture relationships, and opportunities that you would like to attract?

- Are you offering "today's" solutions for your clients? Do you have a strong pulse on what they need and want today?

- Do you find ways to know what is currently going on in your industry, so you can offer relevant and timely solutions to your clients?

- Are you clear on what your "unique selling position" is?

- Have you mapped out what your client's experience looks like when working with you from beginning to end?

- Are your service offerings, products, programs, and marketing implementation plans consistent with your brand?

- How often do you conduct a personal marketing and brand audit on whether or not your messaging, activities, and desired results are aligned with your brand goals?

About Kimberly Pitts

Kimberly Pitts is both a Branding & Marketing Strategist and Developer. She is dedicated to helping entrepreneurial women use branding and marketing strategies to position their businesses in the market, attract their target audiences, create influential brands, realize more income, and enjoy freedom in both their businesses and their lives. She does this through her premier training based mastermind program—Thrive Academy, Branding VIP Program, Packaged for Growth Annual Conference, and a myriad of ongoing training programs.

Anything but conventional, Kimberly is here to provide expert coaching and mentoring to better position you and your business for greater influence.

Learn More Here:
UImpact.net

Continue the Conversation on . . .

Facebook: Facebook.com/UImpact
Twitter: Twitter.com//Uimpact

Chapter 4

Maximum Influence:
Three U's of the Triple Crown
by Alexis M. Scott

Two people traveled to a town to sell their merchandise. One person sold umbrellas and the other person sold sunglasses. The umbrella salesperson had a suitcase filled with samples. The samples included umbrellas in all colors, shapes, and sizes and a myriad of fabrics and styles. That salesperson had the most awesome presentation, as well as a newly developed revolutionary umbrella that beat all other umbrellas.

The other salesperson had a suitcase full of samples of sunglasses in all shapes and colors, with brown tinted lenses and grey tinted lenses. That salesperson had the most awesome presentation and not only a stylish set of lenses, but sunglasses that were truly innovative in how they protected a person's eyes from sunlight.

The town they traveled to was located in an area where six months out of the year there is constant rainfall and six months out of the year there is predominantly sunshine.

Which person do you suppose was in the better position to sell their merchandise? Both salespeople had good products. They both had ideas that were transformative. However, depending on when the rainfall or the sunshine happened, one person would be in a slightly better position than the other. Had either person done their research, they would have been able to determine when the best time would be for them to enter the town to sell their merchandise.

What do you think of when you see the word *position*? There are several meanings to this word. Random House defines position as the following:

1. The location or place of a person or thing at a given moment

2. The way at which a person or thing is placed or arranged

3. The proper or usual place

4. One's stand or opinion

5. One's social standing

6. A post of employment

I prefer a combination of the first two definitions. Position is the way a person or thing is placed or arranged at a given moment. How are you positioning your business for that particular moment? This given moment can catapult your business to the next level, keep your business stagnant, or sink your business to a lower depth. For the two traveling salespeople above, if the umbrella salesperson hit the town during the sunny season, it is doubtful she would sell many umbrellas. She may sell a few, but not as many as she would if she arrived in the town closer to the rainy season. If she was positioned well, then during the next rainy season, the townspeople would remember her for future sales and would always consider her for umbrellas. Similarly, if the sunglass salesperson appeared during the rainy season, it is doubtful that the townspeople would be in the mood to purchase sunglasses in the midst of all the rain. If the sunglass salesperson understood her market, she would enter the town closer to the sunny season.

Does this sound familiar? You have your company name. You have your company idea. You have placed an ad in all major known publications. You have spread your net wide because you want to reach everyone. You have your company product and/or service. You've created your logo and you have your website. You launch your business and sit back and wait for the profits to come streaming in. Week one, you have a slight return on your investment and you predict that by week two, everything is going to happen. Month one, you become a little concerned, but not by much. You are seeing something coming in, but it is $1/1000^{th}$ of what you were expecting. At the six-month mark, you are becoming a little disillusioned. The clients are not knocking down the door as expected. Your grand idea, product, or service is not bringing in the big bucks. At the year mark, you are completely flabbergasted and continually wondering if you should continue. What went wrong?

Or, you have an established business at least two years old. You have been bringing in a steady income. You see some profits but you feel in your heart there is so much more you could be doing. You believe there are more gains you should be receiving. You want your business to transition into a bigger arena. You are not quite sure what steps to take to get there. What must you do?

It is all about positioning—how well you have positioned your business and yourself. Is your business positioned in the right area or to the right people?

Getting the best position can be divided into three categories: **Understanding**, **Uniqueness**, and **Ubiquity**. These three categories will show how you can position your business to:

- Rise to a new level

- Boost from a plateau to the next level

- Achieve the most effective start

Understanding

The first step in positioning your business is to understand your market. In order to understand your market, you must do a fair amount of research. Research other companies that are doing what you are doing or what you want to do. We live in the age of technology which makes the Internet your best friend. Pick your favorite search engine, type in keywords that relate to your product or service and start reading and taking notes. Discover as many business models as you can. Not to mimic (see uniqueness) but to understand. Visit the library. Yes, the Internet is your best friend, but we cannot forget about the libraries. There is much material available on the Internet but not *all* material is available there. Fill in the blanks with a trip to the library. Seek out professional journals for your market. Many of these industry association journals, publications, and past media clips have a cost if you attempt to access them via the Internet. At the library, these publications are free. This research will help you to identify and understand your *whos, whats, wheres,* and *whys.*

The Who

Who are you targeting? If your answer to this question is *everyone*, then you're positioning yourself for disappointment. You do not completely understand your market or ideal client. Research will allow you to be more specific and better position yourself around the right clients for your business. If you have a dog sitting service, you want to target people who have dogs. It will not do your business any good to position yourself amongst people who are not fond of dogs. Remember these people are *everyone*. There is just no feasible way you can reach everyone. When you minimize your market as specifically as possible to a demographic, you can make a more focused position. It is easier to focus on a smaller group and expand out than to find that one perfect needle in the proverbial haystack. For your dog sitting services, you can start your demographic with *everyone*, however do not stop there. Separate everyone into two groups: those with pets and those without pets. What type of pets do these people have? Target those people who have dogs as pets. There are several different dog breeds. What specific breed of dog are you targeting? Do you want small, medium, or large dogs? You can minimize this to a very precise market. You will be better able to tailor your product or service to them. I am not saying that you will not grow. Obviously, we go into business to grow. By positioning yourself within a specific area, your business will grow intelligently, and not sporadically hitting and missing your target. In the long run, you will see a better return on your investment when you make your market as specific as possible. It will save you a lot of money and time.

The Where

Once you gain an understanding of who you are positioning to, position your business to *where* they are. This is another reason why your target cannot be *everyone*. You and your business can't realistically position yourself everywhere. However, you can position yourself and your business in places where your specific target client is located. Your research will highlight those areas. What magazines or journals do your clients read? What conferences or trade shows do your clients attend? Your research will help you to discover these. Even if you cannot be everywhere, you will want the appearance of being everywhere within your specific area (see ubiquity). For your dog sitting service, position your marketing materials where people with dogs frequent (i.e. parks, pet stores, veterinarian's offices). Place an ad in pet magazines. Target the magazines that are distributed in areas where your clients frequent. Place your materials where these people will see and be constantly thinking about you, your product, or your service.

The What

Understanding your market will help you get to the *what* in your business. What product or service are you selling? Clearly knowing this will help in your positioning. Has this product or service already saturated the market? What will make your product   or service noticeable? (See uniqueness.)

The Why

You need to understand why you created your business. This understanding is twofold. Once you completely understand your *why*, you will be better able to explain to your client why they should choose you.

When I started in my business, I would give a version of the following story:

I have been teaching and tutoring math for over twenty years. I started tutoring math in college and continue my entire undergraduate career, either individually or in the math lab. After I received my undergraduate degree, I proceeded to graduate school where I continued to tutor math in that math lab. In addition to the tutoring, I started teaching my own class (assistant to a professor). It was in this process that the teaching bug really hit. I enjoyed being in front of the classroom and working with the students. It was a rush to have students come up to me afterwards and say they finally understood, or mention that they "get it" when there were struggles before. Somehow, I developed the gift of making math palatable and getting students to grasp the concepts.

After graduate school, I started my first job in the "real world" as an engineer. Even though I enjoyed what I was doing, there was something missing. I didn't feel completely fulfilled. I should have been happy but I wasn't. It took me a while to figure out what was missing. Then, I realized I felt this way because I wasn't teaching math. So in my second year of my very first job in the real world, I began looking for part-time teaching positions at local colleges in the area. I would work at my full-time engineering job during the day and teach college math courses in the evening and weekends. And it was great. I continued this trend for fourteen years. The engineering jobs and colleges varied, but I managed to maintain a full-time job during the day and teach on the weekends or in the evenings.

As with everything in life, there was change. Technology entered and more students were opting for the convenience of computer-led instruction over instructor-led instruction. Students were not as willing to attend a weekend course (by then the only course that I was available to teach) as they were previously. To keep pace with technology, the college where I was currently teaching began transitioning away from weekend courses. The "happiness" I had experienced for fifteen or so years was now threatened. However, this change brought an opportunity into my life that completely changed my thought process. It began with friends, family, and co-workers that I had discussions with who mentioned the struggles their children were having with their math courses. Adult students were having some issues returning to school to obtain a degree or additional degree having never fully grasped math. This prompted me to begin individual tutoring.

While I was doing this unofficial tutoring, that candle that was lit over fifteen years prior started to flicker again. The initial joy I had when I stood in front of my first class returned. It really hit me. This is what I should be doing. I needed to help students understand material, alleviate frustrations (because there is a lot), and comprehend the basics. So I decided I wanted to help students firm up their math foundation and overcome their math anxiety and math block. I wanted to instill confidence as they began to embrace math concepts.

When I tell my story, a rapport is developed between my potential clients and me. A connection is formed. When my clients understand my *why*, they are more able to relate to me and more apt to take advantage of what my business has to offer. Being relatable is a good positioner. Therefore, as an entrepreneur, you must understand your why so your clients can have a connection to you. Understanding your why enables you and your business to be positioned with the clients who relate well to you.

The Competition

Finally, your research will show you your competition. As an entrepreneur, you must embrace and understand your competition. Healthy competition helps entrepreneurs build their businesses. Without competition, businesses become stagnant and do not attempt new and diverse innovations.

Competition can be *directly* related to your business—where you and your competition are selling similar services or products, or it can be *indirectly* related to your business—where your competition is not providing the same product or service as you but they are marketing to the same clientele. Your position will be based on how well you understand both types of competitors. Purpose to understand your competition and what people are saying about them—both good things and bad. Look for ways your business can use this information. In terms of the negative feedback concerning your competitors, how can your business leverage this information? In terms of what your competitors do well, how can your business put a different spin on the positive information and use this to your advantage?

While understanding how your competition is positioned, you will receive important information in how to position *your* business. Once you understand your competition, you can develop your uniqueness.

Uniqueness

As a result of your research in your market, you will notice common themes. The next step in positioning yourself is uniqueness. How are you going to do things differently from your competitors? Why would clients want to choose you? This can be difficult at times because as a result of your research, you will notice there are many people who have a product or service similar to yours. The idea may have appeared original in your mind but after performing research, you will see that many people will have had some analogous version of your idea, product, or service. So what is unique about your product or service? Or what can you do to make your product or service unique? Your research is twofold.

Once you have found the commonalities, discover the one different thing and expand on this knowledge to improve your business. If there are twenty active dog sitting services, how do you make your dog sitting service different? You could add a spa service for the dogs, or you could offer a free sitting session for every fifth paid session.

Look at yourself. We are all unique beings. Bring a part of yourself into your positioning. Once you understand your why, use that unique story to speak to your future client. This brings people to you as they relate to your story. When I began in my business, I gave the previous story. My story put a personal spin on my product and services. Always strive to be your authentic self.

Get feedback from your current clients and potential clients. Ask them what they see lacking? What are they receiving or not receiving? Once you get an understanding of the lacks, develop your own distinctive solutions within your business.

Customer Service and Convenience

Make exemplary customer service your standard. With so many similar products and services, excellent customer service is a good differentiator. Show gratitude to the clients you receive the most business from. Offer them something for free that will show your appreciation. Solve problems immediately. Do not give the impression of avoidance. Your clients will appreciate expedient resolutions versus seeing their concerns ignored.

Another way to further your position by uniqueness is to make your product or service convenient. How convenient can you make your product or service to your client? Offer a variety of ways your client can access you, your service or your product. For your dog sitting service, you can offer the convenience of picking up the dogs, versus having the client bring them to you.

Pricing

Many people incorrectly assume that the lowest price is the best, and that it will bring uniqueness to your business. This will bring uniqueness, but not the type of uniqueness you are seeking. Too low of a price may make your product or service appear cheap, or worse, make you unable to sustain your business. The best thing to do with your unique pricing is to show your clients all they will receive with the price of your product or service. Your client will appreciate the value. For your dog sitting service, let's say you offer a service for fifty dollars per day which includes not only sitting but a small groom of your pet. Compare this pricing with a competitor who only dog sits for that same fifty dollars per day. You will stand out more with your price because you have provided something unique in addition to the basic service. If your potential client sees the best value (not necessarily the cheapest), that can strengthen your position.

My Road to Uniqueness— Foundation

One of the main challenges I needed to overcome was to identify something different about myself. So I did a lot of research and I talked with many of my clients and potential clients to see what they were seeking. Many of them were concerned their children did not understand the material and were just being pushed along in the classes. The students were struggling with the tests and receiving poor scores. When I began working with many of the students, I noticed the foundation was shaky. I also noticed this with my college students. The foundation was shaky or completely missing. One of my unique positions was to focus on building a strong foundation. As an entrepreneur, you need to interact with your potential clients. See the concerns and needs and highlight something unique about your product or service that will help your clients recognize you.

Client Discussions

My business began as a basic tutoring service. The only problem with this idea is that after I performed my research, I noticed there were several businesses providing a tutoring service. So I had to think of a way to distinguish myself from this competition. Talking to others helped me realize another unique position that I had. I had a passion for education and I truly wanted the students to learn. This passion was lacking in other tutoring services as they were more focused on getting the highest scores or the best grades. Finally, my clients were a little frustrated by the sizeable amount of money they had to pay for a tutor. They were not seeing any value in the expense. Even though my price was not the cheapest, I explained to my clients the value they would receive from using my service. I offered them something my competitors were not offering . . . a solution that was not a quick fix.

Altering Basic Service and Adding a Team

As my business position grew, I realized I could no longer handle by myself the amount of clients I was getting. I knew clients liked when I tutored, but I could not be everywhere. I began to record the lessons and distribute them online. This allowed people to find me and see my unique style. Always be open to other avenues to provide uniqueness in your business. You may have to alter the presentation of your product or service slightly to further advance your position.

Another way for me to reach more clientele was to grow a team. My team includes a group of people who value education and want the students to succeed. Students can feel when their needs are not being valued. They can see through the façade of their educators. Every one I have chosen has a love and a desire to teach. The people you hire for your team should reflect your unique style. They are representations of your company.

Ubiquity

When we were discussing *"The Where,"* I mentioned that you cannot realistically be everywhere. However, with ubiquity, you can have the appearance of being everywhere within your specific market. This will take your position well beyond the next level.

When I suggest ubiquitousness, I am *not* suggesting you run around sporadically attending every event, or place ads in every publication. This approach will cost you a lot of time and money and you are not likely to see a positive return on this investment. What I am suggesting is a more tactical approach. Start out by having conversations with others who are currently in your market. This discussion with your competitors and mentors will assist you in making your approach more direct. Competitors and mentors will be able to share lessons learned. They can tell you which publications are the best to advertise in or which conferences you should attend. Someone may have already gone through what you are attempting and can prevent you from making a costly mistake.

Credibility and Character

We discussed customer service in the *"Uniqueness"* section. Credibility and character go hand in hand with customer service. Yes, you do want to have a positive appearance of being everywhere. However, you do not want your ubiquity position to be tarnished with negative actions.

What do you want to be known for when you position yourself? Do you want to be known for failure to follow through with your commitments? Do you want to be known for being indifferent to your client's concerns? Do you want to be known for not reaching your clients in the agreed upon time? That is a sure way to lower your position in your client's eyes. Do what you say you will do. Be positively consistent. One of my best traits is my punctuality. That is because I value my time and my client's time. If you talk to any of my clients they will tell you I am always there when I am supposed to be. When talking with future clients, my reputation for punctuality was already there and many appreciated it.

Referrals and Testimonials

Get your clients to refer you. It is perfectly okay to ask for the referral. If your clients sincerely like your product or service, they will be more than happy to refer you. They will keep your name out there. Think about it. When you find a product you really enjoy, what do you do? You tell everyone. This concept also works for you as an entrepreneur. Word-of-mouth can be the best positioner. Reward the clients who refer you. Your unique customer service will make your current clients want to refer you. Several of my first clients were word-of-mouth referrals. People who appreciated what I did were not hesitant to spread the word.

Ask your clients to write a testimonial or record a video testimonial. Place these testimonials on your website, in your newsletter, on your blog, in your printed marketing material, or as status updates in your social media. Getting others talking about you adds to your ubiquity. I repeat. Positive word-of-mouth will assist you in achieving a strong position. Just like with referrals, do not be afraid to ask your clients to write a testimonial about the service they received from you.

Social Media

Social media allows you to promote your name, idea, product, or service. Social media permits you to demonstrate your expertise in the market and build relationships between you and your client. Social media also allows you to get client feedback through client interactions. Social media allows you to reach a large number of clients without actually physically being in those specific areas. You can use the expanse of the Internet to spread your message.

Networking, Trade Shows, Conferences

Go where your clients go. Attend major conferences or trade shows where potential clients are apt to attend. Do not try to attend *all* of these events, but intelligently select the top five where you feel you will make the greatest impression. Networking is necessary. In order to obtain ubiquity, you must get out and talk to others about your business. Using others via referrals and testimonials is great. This is your business and ultimately, you need to promote it.

Presentations

Have a few events to launch your product or service or see if you could give a presentation at a conference. This will allow people to meet you personally and relate to you. To be honest, when you first start out, you may not have a huge attendance at your events. Use these initial events to polish your presentation. Make it as perfect as possible, so that when you are able to get a larger audience or present at a conference/trade show, you have the best presentation. The people you need to meet will be at these events. All you really need is that one connected person to see your presentation or hear of how great your presentation is.

Record a presentation about your product or service. Distribute snippets of your presentation on your website or in your newsletter. Even if your audience is not in front of you, they can view your presentation at their leisure. If people enjoy what they've seen, they will share your presentation with others and attempt to see your full presentation live.

Those small attended events will grow based on this recorded presentation. These presentations will provide a continued presence or ubiquity.

Business Associations

Visit and join your local Chamber of Commerce. This is great for getting and keeping your name out there. Make a visit to your local Visitor's Bureau. Some visitor's bureaus will allow you to market your materials. Many new visitors to your city frequent these bureaus and can see your name and consider your product or service. Visit your local Small Business Association. They are not only there to help you in your business but they are an excellent source to provide referrals to your business, or to be a referrer for your business.

Newsletter

A periodic newsletter will help with ubiquity in your position. Putting out a newsletter increases your visibility and your credibility. You are positioning yourself as an expert for your service or your product. You are giving your opinion and providing your clientele with information they may not have received before. Allow your clients to forward your newsletter to anyone they feel will benefit. The more you make yourself, your product, or your service have the appearance of being everywhere, the better your position will be to gain the clientele in your specific area.

Collaboration

Collaborate with others in your market or tangential to your market. For your dog sitting service, you can partner with someone who has a cat sitting service or someone who house sits. Even though their market is not specifically dogs, they may be able to refer people to you from their market who would have the dogs for which you would pet sit. In this collaboration however, do not always take. Offer something in return to your collaborators that will assist them in their business. Be very genuine with this offer.

Our umbrella and sunglass salespeople went back to their respective offices to strategize. They began to research the town and truly understand what the people who lived there needed. They discovered the best time for each of them to enter the town. Even though they had unique ideas about their respective products, their research uncovered that many of the townspeople were looking for more practical umbrellas and more stylish sunglasses. The townspeople were also very turned off by the customer service received from their current sunglasses/umbrella salespeople. They wanted people who provided superior customer service. Our salespeople started separate social media sites and began discussing the benefits of their respective products, displaying their merchandise on their individual sites and inviting the townspeople to comment and give their opinions on the products. Our salespeople distributed monthly newsletter both in the on-season and off-season, so the townspeople would constantly have the sunglasses and umbrellas on their minds even though they were seasonal. The umbrella salesperson and the sunglass salesperson began to collaborate; each agreeing to be a reference for the other when they entered the town, to maintain ubiquity. Any time a townsperson bought a pair of sunglasses, they would receive a discount on an umbrella (and vice versa). Each salesperson improved their position in the eyes of the townspeople and as a result, increased their sales.

In summary, to improve your business position in your market or to make that preeminent start, you must:

- ***Understand* your market**—research, research, research.

- **Be *unique* in your market**—find and feature your differences.

- ***Be ubiquitous* in your market**—even though you cannot sensibly be everywhere, have the appearance of being everywhere.

Happy and Effective Positioning!

About Alexis M. Scott

Alexis M. Scott is a Triple E: *Educator*, Entrepreneur, and *Engineer*. She founded AMS Academic Solutions in order to share her gift of numbers and education that she has possessed since an early age. She has been teaching mathematics for over twenty years including eighteen years as a college professor. She currently lives in Dallas, TX and in her spare time enjoys playing tennis.

Contact Alexis at alexis@amsacademicsolutions.com

Learn More Here:
Amsacademicsolutions.com

Continue the Conversation on . . .

Facebook: Facebook.com/AMathServices
Twitter: Twitter.com/AlexisMath22

Chapter 5

Identifying and Owning Your Entrepreneurial Super Powers
by Andrea Sullenger

Finding Your Inner Super Hero

Creating your dream entrepreneurial experience is predicated on you establishing your own unique entrepreneur identity. It is about you laying claim to how you want to be seen and heard, how you want to serve the world, and what makes you different than all the others. Establishing your strength of position in the vast oasis of the entrepreneurial wonderland is all about you choosing, identifying, leveraging, capitalizing, and becoming more visible. I call this, "finding your inner super hero." Super heroes have been known for their strength, extraordinary super-human like gifts, talents, powers, and they always possess audacious fearlessness. To thrive as an entrepreneur you have to do the same. I realize that you may not think you are a great comparison to a super hero right now; maybe you don't enter your office each day wearing red and white knee high boots, a blue, red and gold star studded leotard, and a groovy gold starred headband, but you do have super hero powers. Let me break it down and show you how to access them and in return you will gain positioning strength inside of your target market.

Positioning is all about choosing how you become seen and known to your perfect audience and your networking partners. It is the deployment of you placing yourself into perfect visibility to create the business you desire. Building the right positioning for yourself isn't about doing business as usual or about following the rules. If you want to create high impact positioning, you have to decide that you will be the one to write your own rules. You be the author of your path. People are desperate to see, relate, and follow someone that can do exactly that. When you write your own rules and carve out your sweet spot, you create engagement, a following, and a confidence others will have for you and your work. Positioning isn't something you can purchase from an online program, a book, a workshop, a certification, or degree. Positioning comes from you choosing it, going after it, and claiming it until your work and name are so big and impactful that you no longer need to introduce yourself.

There are several key components you have to identify prior to establishing your positioning stance. First, who is your target market and what unique value do you bring to them, or what is your niche? I subscribe to the philosophy that the people you serve are your target market and the value you bring to them is your niche. If you are unclear about either aspect, you must STOP now, work it out, and then continue. There is no way to reputably create strength of position if you are not clear as to whom you serve and how. Allow me to offer a few queries that may help you flesh it out so it is clearer for you:

- Who do you find great connection with? (what group of people)

- Who inspires you?

- Who are you forever curious about?

- What fascinates you about this group of people or their work?

- When you are working with them do you lose track of time?

- Does it feel more like play than work when you are surrounded by them?

- How does it feel to be with this group of people? Notice I said *feel*.

When you are narrowing down and laying stake to your perfect target market, you must find a core group of people who bring you internal joy, and fan the flame of inspiration and curiosity within. If that is not what you are feeling about the target market you serve or have claimed, it is possible you selected them based off of logic rather than passion. I find that entrepreneurs who select based on logic become uninspired themselves . . . bored, resentful, and exhausted. You want to show up with energy and a longing to pour your heart and soul into your service and therefore you have to—no, you need pursue working with those who fill you up, and call to your passions.

Your niche is simply how you serve your target market. Delivery of service can show up in a multitude of ways and there isn't a set right or wrong way to do this. However, you do need to understand the needs and wants from your target market. Usually, entrepreneurs get caught up in this piece of the puzzle—the simpler, the "how to," the one-two-three steps.

It is more systematic and makes sense. *"I provide this, for this amount of time, and I deliver it this way."* I think there is more to it. I dare you to let go of the linear way of thinking through how you will deliver your work and try to think about the emotions behind and under your target client's challenge and the break-through they are desperate to unearth. Think about the transformational feeling, energy, and result you want them to feel and be able to express at the end of working with you. I believe you will craft a better and more complete understanding of your target market, their urgent challenge, and the soul-longing transformation that must take place for you to gain powerful positioning with them and their network.

How will you know if the target market and your initial niche are a perfect match right out of the gate? Chances are you won't. Chances are as you grow the business and yourself, your understanding and knowledge will evolve. As you grow, your focus and attention will become tightened. Most entrepreneurs are held captive in the beginning from fear of selecting the wrong target market, the wrong niche, and not being able to deliver high quality service, so they cast the net wide. They are so afraid of excluding someone or some group that they want to include everyone. Reality is, you can't be profound and effective by working with or serving everyone. Your message becomes lost. The best way for you to *not* get stuck in the crevasse of fear and avoid *not* claiming your place in a market is to simply decide what you want. Write it out. You don't have to have all of the answers right this moment, you just have to choose to begin. After you have chosen you can spend some intentional time researching the details and laying the foundation for what your target market and niche will really shake out to be. One word of caution here, don't allow your inner censor to squash your vision. Your seedling ideas may not work out completely how you have pictured them but they are most likely extending from an inner connectedness. They are most likely bubbling to the surface because they call to who you really are, who you really enjoy working and being with, and to your innate skills, gifts, and talents. The inner censor will tell you things like, *"No one has ever done that before so chances are it won't work."* Or, *"Is that really acceptable?"* Or, *"What makes you think you could add value to that group of people?"* . . . and so much more. Silence the inner censor (which we all have). Tell her to shut the hell up and then continue to immerse yourself in the choosing of who and how you will serve the world. Take the next step and do your homework. Research eight to ten entrepreneurs that cater to your ideal target market. What value do they bring to them? What is the niche they possess? Take a look at the language they use on their website, social media, and any marketing collateral. Through the written words they use you may be able to identify details about the target market you missed, their core challenge and need, and the transformation that they can expect to gain by working with that company and entrepreneur. This exercise isn't meant for you to fall prey to copying what others in the same or similar market are doing. Nor is it a shot for you to beat yourself up about how much farther they are down the rabbit trail than you. This is simply research, idea stimulating research.

New entrepreneurs are coming onto the scene all the time, literally daily. Some come in and go out in the same day while others create massive waves and build ridiculously amazing followings. Why? Aren't we all faced with the task of sculpting our uniqueness and rising above the noise and competition? Truth is, we are. So why is it that some make it and others don't? I think it simple really, I think some actually believe they've now entered some competitive race, and when they see it's a marathon and not a sprint, or that hundreds who started sooner are ahead of them, they bail. If some can come in "late" and craft successful businesses with massive impact, then it only proves there is no competition outside of oneself. The confrontation we face is the discovery of what makes us unique. What sets you apart from others inside of the same target market? Clarity is power, so let's get clear about your unique gifts and talents. Take out a sheet of paper and write down as many things as you can think of at which you are really great—things you do well. These things don't have to be solely geared towards the entrepreneurial endeavor you are adventuring towards. Next, list the things that excite your soul and you absolutely love doing. Now ask twenty five friends to tell you the things they believe are your greatest strengths or talents. How do the lists meet up? Do you see some common words or phrases that keep popping up for people? How could these strengths translate into value extended and given to   your ideal target market?

Remember, I said positioning isn't something that happens to you. Positioning is something you construct. Once the foundation of who you are and how you show up in the entrepreneurial wonderland, and who and how you serve is defined, then you can be confident it is time for you to do what I call, "take the stage." Have you ever been to a concert for a famous rock and roller? The concerts I have been to don't seem to have someone announcing who will be coming on stage. In my experience, the energy is high, the stadium goes dark, the music blasts and the performers and the band burst onto the stage, lights illuminate, and they powerfully enter into their work, their first song. Sure, there is some guy back stage that says *ok go on now*," but there is no big announcement. Why? Because we, the attendees, are in the audience waiting with anticipatory excitement to be given an incredible show. The world is also waiting for this. There are millions and millions of people out there waiting for you to storm the stage and give them a show. I am the stage manager and I am telling you, *"It is time to go on!"* How do you "take the stage"? You do it like a rock star, that's how. You grab hold of your unique talents, gifts, and your network, and you go give it away. I don't necessarily mean you give it away for free, but in some cases that actually will be true. It is your time to build your platform and position. There are a hundred and one ways to create visibility. The main thing is that you select two or three of them, and implement them right away. One of the things I do to set myself apart and to create authority, credibility, engagement, and visibility is to play the role of interviewer. I do an interview series where I showcase powerful, creative, and inspiring women entrepreneurs. This one stage-taking activity instantly creates connection, places me in the role of professional, and lends me the opportunity to work from a place of credibility. Come up with a list of ways you can "take the stage" and begin building your powerful positioning this week.

Birthing your best business and life isn't easy. Most of the time it isn't fast either. However, you can build the perfectly matched business and life. One that offers external and internal rewards beyond your wildest dreams if you are willing to do the work; if you are willing to get out of your own way and out of your own head where that internal censor lives. If you are willing to tap into your own super hero powers and shine the spotlight onto them for the world to see. In this chapter, I have given you the exercises to work through to find your super hero powers. Super heroes have confidence, strength, and a desire to help others. All of that is also true to who you are at your core. To be an extraordinary entrepreneur you have to dig deep and pull up that internal confidence, and strength, and find who you have a passion to help. The only thing remaining is you donning the cape and boots, and charging the stage.

Mindful and Courageous Engagement

In a world where doing more in less time, "faster is better," and non-stop communication through technology trumps face-to-face connection, the art of mindful and courageous engagement has become lost. It is a practice that has been pushed to the back seat, maybe even the trunk. As entrepreneurs it is vital for us to course correct and adopt the practice of once again engaging in face-to-face or ear-to-ear relationship building. Let's get honest with one another, no entrepreneur, including me, has ever built anything of significance because we made a vision board, hung out our shingle, and the masses came running. Nope . . . none of us have had it unfold quite like that. The reality is, it takes far more than doing either one of those tasks to attract and create the idea clients—clients who perform at their peak and refer their network.

I have heard it said many times, you have to attract the right clients. While this may be true, I believe it is only a portion of what has to take place in order for you to not only attract, but to impact and gain someone as a trusted client. The attraction piece can be anything from your website, business cards, how you present yourself at a live or virtual networking event, and a hundred additional items. In my book, I share that to attract means to gain someone's attention long enough to personally engage with them and possibly create the ideal client you are looking for. Do you need to have your website and business cards in order? Yes, but do you *have to,* No! I know some entrepreneurs who have the ugliest looking websites and plain Jane business cards—or none at all—and still seem to attract and create their dream clients. How is this possible? Engagement! It is that simple.

I don't know what type of business you want to have or are creating, but chances are you leverage the Internet in some capacity. That's great, but don't get sucked into the belief that you can automate it all, talk to no one, be seen by no one right out of the gate, and still be attracting and creating more clients than you can handle. The guys and gals you read about who share how they are living life to the fullest, working two hours a week with everything else automated, and still raking in a cool million each month didn't start off that way. Believe me. For some of you, working completely automated will never take place because your business is totally based on relationships and interaction. I'm a coach, so this is true for me, and if I decided I didn't want to engage with people, I would soon be living in a box. Not a pretty sight. I am all about automation and leveraging your knowledge, but when it comes to creating new clients, you will be hard pressed to yank yourself out of the mix and still maintain above average results.

Creating clients sounds harder than it is. Creating clients is simply you putting yourself out there and intentionally having the right conversations with networking partners or people who you would love as your clients. Making sure you are clear about who you serve—your target market—and knowing what you offer them is step one. After that it is simply about designing and implementing your reach out campaign. Make a list of potential networking partners. Who do you know or are mildly acquainted with who has access and connection with people who fall into your target market category? Next, simply reach out to them. Do the same with a list of people you can make entitled, *"People I would die to have as my dream clients."* Reaching out takes a spoonful of courage, but honestly, the worst thing that can happen is they don't respond or they do and simply say *"Not right now."* Either way, you will have done the hard part, the first step, the reach out. If they say no, remember you literally have the same thing you had five minutes prior. No guts no glory, right?

When you are engaging with either a networking partner or a potential client, there are so many things you can do wrong and only a few you need to do right. Before I give you the ones you have to get right, I challenge you to take a minute or two and create for yourself an editorial calendar of your daily action for reaching out and engaging with those who can help you create your ideal business. Think about this, you could simply reach out to two people each day, and I don't mean by way of private message on Facebook. Sure, maybe that's how you initially set up a time to connect, but I am referring to actually speaking with two or more people each day, five days a week . . . what power that would have in moving you into the business you really desire. Focus on reaching out to two each day to set up a time to genuinely connect, speaking with two each day, introducing two people from your network to one another each day, and adding value to at least one in your network. Don't mistake the two introductions for referrals, they are not. They are simply you introducing one person to another. It is you taking time to set yourself apart, adding value back into your relationships and networking. Introduce people who have something in common with one another or could benefit from one another. Adding value is easy. Pick one person in your network, maybe someone you have not spoken with in sometime. How could you add value to them today? Maybe send them an interesting article, video, book, or even just a personal note inquiring how their latest project is going. Be the guy or gal who adds value just because it is who you are, not because you are doing it to get something in return. Now, on to the steps you have to "get right" to create your ideal clients, and engage with them courageously and boldly to not just get what you want, but give what they need.

First and foremost, set aside ample time to authentically connect with them. Don't rush the process or behave in a manner that gives off a sense that you are in a hurry. Your focus is to create trusted clients, and you cannot do that in a quick and rushed twenty-minute conversation. I have to say this is a hard one for most of us. Most of us are about doing, accomplishing, and checking off those to-do lists, but these conversations cannot work like that if you want a positive outcome.

Second, come with the attitude and heart to authentically connect with them, and to learn about what is happening in their life and work. This can sometimes be hard when you are anxious to share your own news or if you are chomping at the bit to nail them down as a client, but don't do it. Depending on what you do and offer, it can sometimes take multiple conversations before you loop back around to a sales dialogue.

Third, don't just listen to what they have to share, but really *hear* them. If you are on the phone with them, make a commitment to behave as if they are sitting right in front of you—no multi-tasking here.

Fourth, offer them up an intangible . . . your knowledge. Give them value where you can.

Fifth, after you have connected, you can move into inviting them to share what they need from you and in turn what you need from them. Be specific. Don't say things like, "*Well I can always use another client. Do you know of anyone looking for a___?*" Everyone wants more clients and statements like this don't empower or create willingness from the one you are speaking with. When you are asking for a referral, make it easy. For example, if you sell real estate you might say something like, "*Yes, what I am looking for right now is someone that has a single story home, three bedrooms or more on the south side of town, and is considering selling. I have a family looking to buy, and I just need to find them the perfect home that meets those requirements. Do you know anyone thinking of selling on the south side or anyone on the south side who has a single story home? I would be honored if you could connect us.*" When you make the invitation and the request very specific, you make it easy for them to think of who they know and connect the dots. I also like to email my specific invitation request so it is top-of-mind awareness.

Sixth, if they are the ideal client, or if after we connect they fit what I am looking for and they say "*Yes that's me,*" I slow it down again. I don't pounce and say "*Great, I'll send over the payment link now.*" I confirm what they want, why they want it, and if they did take me up on my offer, what their greatest outcome would be. If that is smooth sailing, then I can move into the sales piece but remember, sometimes you only get to step five, or sometimes you get through step six but they are not ready to commit. That is ok. Don't just say goodbye. Ask when you can follow up, and then do that. You may have to start at step one again, or you may find you are somewhere in the middle or at step five again. In all cases, it is okay. When you are making a sale or gaining a new client you have to remember that the choice for them always falls into where they are in life at that very moment.

For me as a coach, the engagement process is vital to creating and establishing solid relationships and expectations with my clients before we even begin our work together.

Sometimes I connect and engage with potential clients only to weed them out as I learn and find that they really are not who I would like to work with. Other times I connect and engage with them multiple times because of where they are in life. Engagement should be your number one marketing activity and you should be spending eighty percent of your time on it each week. It is also the hardest piece of what you will do. It is a process, but if you can learn to master it and to harness the power in building relationships, you and your business will soar with every courageous and bold connection, and with the engagement you have with possible clients.

"Think twice before you speak, because your words and influence will plant the seed of either success or failure in the mind of another." -Napoleon Hill

Own It

Own it. Those are the words I had to tell myself early on in my entrepreneurial adventure. I for sure was *not* an expert, I for sure didn't feel very influential, and I was shaking in my boots most of the time. Even sometimes now, I will take on a client or a project that scares me to death. I have learned, when I feel like that, it means I am on the right path. It also means I have to repeat, *"Own it, own it, own it,"* over and over and over again. Becoming influential doesn't mean you fake it until you make it or that you wait until someone tells you that you are now influential. Becoming influential in your niche means staying the course for the long haul. It means proving yourself many times over. It means staying in a place where you are constantly learning, willfully sharing that knowledge with others, and it means you do "it" anyway, afraid or not. When you can become known as a giver, not a taker or a matcher, but as a servant driven, highly competent and integrity filled person in your area of expertise, then you get passed the crown and scepter of "influencer."

The piece that trips up most entrepreneurs as they build their influential reach is the, "staying for the long haul." I am sure this can be attributed to many things but the two I see most often are, lack of planning—expectations are out of control and not on a realistic time frame, and not entering into entrepreneurship understanding the gigantic mental hurdles they will be faced with daily. My advice is for you to plan everything out, all the details, and give yourself double the time you think it will take to implement and to reap the rewards, and make a commitment to stay the course. One way you can do this is to invest in your personal development. Make a plan of how you will do this each month, each quarter and each year. Which books will you read? Which workshops, retreats, or seminars will you attend? Do you need a mentor or coach?

What scares you, but you know it is necessary to gain credibility and influence in your niche and with your target market? Okay, do that! When was the last time you did that or anything close to it? Take public speaking, for example. It is something that is a huge fear for most people. However, it is also one of the best ways for you to be seen and heard as an expert in your field. It offers a chance for you to begin to give away your knowledge, your unique perspective on specific information that pertains to your target market. It is an opportunity to build that influence muscle until it is so big they can't ignore it.

Becoming an "influencer" is a choice. It is you deciding to stay the course and do the things that make you scared, in spite of the fear. It is you pushing through the rough patches, doing the personal development, and keeping up on what is working and what isn't in your niche, and it is you owning your dream and telling anyone who questions it to either get in the arena with you or keep their opinion to themselves. It is you owning that you have a voice and a message that only you can deliver to the world. Becoming an "influencer" isn't for the faint of heart, it is for those who are willing to dig deep, find their inner super hero powers, fearlessly and courageously engage with the world, and own their message.

I believe in you.

About Andrea Sullenger

Andrea is mix of "kick butt" sales/marketing coach and inspirational possible-i-tarian. She has been working with solo-entrepreneurs for the past seventeen years, helping them build their own thriving businesses all while creating a life they love. Andrea is a nationally known speaker and coach, and an internationally published author. She is a creative, out-of-the-box thinker who will challenge you to go after a BIG life and a BIG business.

Learn More Here:
AndreaSullenger.com

Continue the Conversation on . . .

Facebook: Facebook.com/andreasullengercom

Chapter 6

Win-Win Content Marketing:
Brand Publishing to Lead, Connect, Educate, and Inspire
by Margo DeGange

I am a content publisher, and yes, I am a content marketing and publishing consultant, yet sometimes I just about cringe when I hear the term "content marketing." That's because there is great misunderstanding about the concept, gross misinformation about the purpose, and even "marketing abuse" within the practice of content marketing.

Yet, I can think of no better way to become an influential entrepreneur and position yourself for win-win engagement than to lead boldly with your brand through the publishing of solid content—high quality, desirable content that is engaging, informative, interesting, and reliable.

For certain, publishing quality content entails much more than creating a "piece" or two (or twenty) to get noticed, and it is certainly a far cry from designing a "catchy," "pithy," or "sexy" headline to get the "click" so you can "get the sale!"

In essence, becoming a serious content publisher is more along the lines of becoming an "Influence Marketer," but not in the sense that you use it as a deliberate strategy to get your content in front of the eyes of the *big* influencers (although who would turn that down?). It must be more foundational and sincere than that. As a brand, through persuasive content and brand engagement, you have the astounding opportunity to help shape and influence your community by providing what they want to know more about. You deliver it, and you therefore become "influential." Do you want to become an influential entrepreneur? Then embrace brand publishing to lead, connect, educate, and inspire.

No Longer Mostly About You!

The day is long gone when an entrepreneur can begin a relationship with their party of interest by throwing a few ads out to reel them in and make the sale. Today, the relationship begins well before anyone ever becomes a client. I believe that for the conscious, mission-driven entrepreneur, marketing has been replaced with good communication! Today's purchasers want more than products and services. They want business "relationships" and people they can trust. To gain a client today, you must stand for something he or she resonates with and believes in. You must have a business purpose and brand so meaningful it resonates with the hearts and minds of your prospects, and penetrates their lives!

Shift Your Thinking

The "flavor" of your business cannot be about "selling." If you're to become a publisher of value, you need a shift in thinking. Forget about a content marketing strategy where you exchange words and information for a sale. Instead, devote yourself to being a lifelong contributor of *value*, *meaningful inspiration*, and *relevant information*. It's a business-lifestyle decision; a choice to become a different kind of "marketer."

Begin Everything with a Genuine Mission

Being a quality brand publisher begins with a genuine, meaningful, overwhelming mission that drives you each and every day. If you have that, then everything you do and every bit of content you create becomes a rich, vivid, and sincere expression of that mission, and a means to connect, educate, and inspire through it (which by default is true leadership)!

It's all about perspective. So, rather than springboarding from a set of strategies and tasks you "do" to achieve a sales or marketing goal or objective, as a value publisher, you reach out to the world as an extension of who you "are" to fully live your mission. This definitely beats having an "agenda!"

All you have to do now is decide what you "stand for." What do you (and your brand) represent that won't change when sales are up or down—that will still be your core value message when times get rough or when the floodgates of sales are opened? What are you here to contribute? How can you improve lives, build up others, influence needed change? This is your mission!

Your Underlying Motivation

Be committed to your purpose! In other words, know precisely why your business exists, other than to make a profit, and let *that* be the cause (the story—your brand philosophy) others align with and relate to, and are eager to rally around. Then, you simply communicate, reiterate, demonstrate, substantiate, and authenticate this brand story in all the content you publish. Publishing becomes the *way*.

Who do you influence or impact . . . how, and why? What is the significance of your work to the bigger picture of your life and your life-purpose in general? This is the underlying motivation of your brand that stems directly from you. Intimately know and embrace this motivation, and commit to always serve others from this vantage point.

Is Selling Out of the Question?

You are in business, so of course you must sell products and services, and you must turn a profit. The reality is, your valuable content will help you build a thriving and robust community with people who want to buy from you, but your "motive" must always be one of contribution, and not of sucking people into your "funnel." Create a user experience that is rich with meaning and your brand will become valuable to your audience (community). From there they will *want* to get behind you and even help promote what you do, because they believe in it so strongly. If your purpose rings true to others, they are likely to become your clients and customers.

Show Up as a Leader in Your Content Publishing

A leader is propelled by a solid sense of purpose—that *brand philosophy* and *mission* we addressed earlier. Again, these become the constant "story" those you want to attract are drawn to and inspired by.

You lead by creating and distributing timely, relevant, and useful content that stems from your story and that's designed specifically to help a clearly defined target audience.

As a leader, you know who your special people are. You know them well. You care about them and you fully understand their concerns. You know them so well that you know how to help them get where they need to be. Your story will organically and naturally appeal to them. Through significant content that's important to them, you become someone they want to listen to and of course, follow. You become a trusted and reliable specialist with the advice, resources, and information they need, seek and enjoy. With *your* brand, they never feel they are being "sold to," even when you mention a service or product on occasion. Because you are driven by that compelling mission, they will recognize your expertise, and they will sense from your style that you have their best interests at heart.

Good and Clever Content, but not Mission-Based

As a content publisher (content marketer), your mission will keep you focused. There will be many opportunities for you to publish "good," "clever," or "hot" content. You however, are a leader with a purpose. With your mission ever before your eyes, it will be easy for you to avoid the trends and temptations just to get a few extra "likes" or comments with your content. Stay genuine to what you stand for and true to your community, and your value exchange will stay strong and intact.

Make Content Publishing Your Business Lifestyle

Content publishing is a lifestyle, not a shot-in-the-dark activity. It's not for everyone, but it may be for *you*! Do you want to have true influence in your market niche? Do you want to lead selflessly with a powerful mission that is often communicated though written words? Are you willing to make a commitment to a business-lifestyle that embraces content marketing as a long-term endeavor. It's not the kind of thing you start and stop. So know that going in. Writing a blog post now and then, commenting on social media without being mindful of your business philosophy, publishing an article or report when the "mood" strikes you and without a plan, is quite possibly a total waste of time in terms of influence, and it definitely is not "Influence Marketing!" However, if you think you have what it takes to stay the course, read on. I have some excellent and proven content marketing/publishing tactics and tips you can weave into your master plan, as you see fit, of course!

Some Tactics: *How* You Interact and Share

As a content publisher with a mission, you must create a two-way stream of information. Not only should you communicate value to your community, but they should be encouraged and inspired to communicate their thoughts, ideas, challenges, concerns, and feedback to you. In addition to a content marketing and publishing strategy, you also need specific tactics, information vehicles, and a schedule that works for both you and your community. Choosing these will depend on your goals and available resources, such as time and dollars.

A brand publishing strategy of content marketing involves many channels from which your content can be accessed by others, including (and there are even *more* channels than this):

- Your business card (yes, believe it)

- Your email signature

- Your free gift on your website or landing page

- Your newsletter or ezine

- Your blog

- Your guest blog appearances

- Your interviews

- Your digital or print magazine

- Your articles

- Your guides and reports

- Your speaking (keynotes, breakouts, workshops, speeches, webinars, seminars, and teleseminars)

- Your social media

- Your videos

- Your book

To help you gain influence right away, I want to further address just a few of these channels on the pages that follow: your free gift on a landing page, your newsletter or ezine, your blog, your digital magazine, your social media, and your book (yes, you *can* write and publish a book). With each one, I will give you some tips, highlights, and frequency suggestions for publishing. First, I will briefly discuss the value of an editorial calendar.

Your Editorial Calendar

It's exciting to think that you can be in control of your brand and your content, and strategize the best way to serve your community. Through the use of an editorial calendar, much of your content can be planned and written well in advance, and even pre-scheduled. This helps you take control of your publishing and really brand it to your mission. It also sets the tone for your content pieces to form a cohesive whole. Your editorial calendar helps you see the big picture, publish in a timely manner, factor holidays and special occasions into the mix, and publish consistently across different media. You can even reveal some of your publishing dates in advance to joint-venture partners, or to your tribe members who you know will happily anticipate certain pieces of content.

I personally like to create an editorial calendar for an entire year in advance, planning it and selecting my topics and titles in the fourth quarter of the previous year. Try it. You can always tweak it, and you can and should leave room for a little unexpected copy and some spontaneity, too.

Your *Valuable Free Gift* on a Landing Page

Your *Valuable Free Gift* will be some type of highly useful content that's relevant to your community. It can be anything your target audience finds beneficial, such as a reference guide, a checklist, a report, a *"What to Avoid"* article, or anything to help your community achieve a goal, solve a problem, or gain a desired outcome (choose a name for this gift that clearly represents the benefit).

Create a clean, clutter-free landing page (a signup form displaying only your photo or video, your logo, and the name of the report) and publish it on a domain name that is easy to remember and that also showcases the benefit of the gift, such as "RedesignInAWeekend.com." Since the domain is easy to remember, you can share it online and when you are out and about, effortlessly directing people to gain access to it.

Your *Valuable Free Gift* may just be your first significant opportunity to begin a one-on-one relationship with your prospect; and communicate a clear and meaningful message and purpose tied to your story and brand. Show up here as a knowledgeable, connected leader.

✓ **Publishing Frequency:** "Tweak," or even completely change out your *Valuable Free Gift* yearly, as you revisit your brand, mission, and the direction of your business.

Your Newsletter or Ezine

Your newsletter (also called an ezine) is a tried-and-true way to publish regular content your community can count on. As basic as it is, it's a solid touch point, and it shocks me to discover that so many people think newsletters are "old news" or no longer a viable communication tool. It may be one of your *best*! It is permission-based and more intimate than many other forms of communication.

With newsletters, it's vital to keep them short, sweet, and interesting. Create punchy but *authentic* subject lines (notice I did not say "gimmicky") that are so related to the goals and desires of your community, they get excited to read your correspondence. Include an article, a tip, your photo, and a short bio. You can also keep subscribers up to date on events of interest. Add social media share buttons and a "forward to a friend" link. In each issue, include a link to your blog with a standing invitation to visit it often.

✓ **Publishing Frequency:** Weekly, and plan the year's topics, tips, and images in advance on your editorial calendar.

Your Blog

Your blog is where you can shine as a leader, and through it you can become a notable resource for your community, bringing them back to you over and over again, while giving them tremendous value. Let your unique personality and brand shine though your posts, while being interesting, informative, and educational, and throw some fun in from time to time as well!

As a leader in your field, publish a variety of content types, including innovative or useful ways of doing something, your thoughts on news and current issues important to your community (since you *are* an opinion leader), tips to make the readers' lives easier, interesting facts your target audience will enjoy, information about upcoming events, reviews and links to valuable resources, pertinent lifestyle information, and even a testimonial on occasion (particularly if it demonstrates how someone gained a definite solution to a problem).

I highly recommend Wordpress as your blog platform, as it is SEO-friendly and allows you to have a blog right on your website—even on your home page—if you prefer it that way. Wordpress also allows you to set up custom categories, so organizing your published content is a breeze and very user-friendly. When your site visitors search for specific content, they can pull it up either by key word or category. I suggest setting up between five and eight categories that correlate to the major topics of interest of your target audience. Then, each time you write a post, you can assign it to a category. This is a win-win for you and your community, as it helps you to focus when you write, and it makes finding relevant content easy for the visitor.

It is easy to create a good blog post, so don't get stuck on it. You can pull excerpts from previous articles you've written, or even expand a bit on an intriguing social media comment you made (I do this all the time). Simply rework the content so it's not identical to what you've posted previously.

Visuals are great. A wonderful tool for adding cool visuals to your blog is SlideShare.net. It is an online viewer that can be embedded into a blog post (or web page). Simply upload your slides (that already reside somewhere on your PC or Mac) and share them online. Let the slides tell the information or story.

Written blog posts are best when they are short and to the point, as attention is hard to keep these days. Skip the "filler." Create clear, informative "blurbs" of rock-solid content in line with your brand philosophy (your story) and rich in usefulness for the reader. Keep each post to about 250-300 words. Add a related image, too, which captures further interest. Oh, and every blog post should have convenient social media buttons for easy sharing.

✓ **Publishing Frequency:** Weekly at first. Once you are steady and consistent, you may choose to increase to twice weekly or more, as long as you can be consistent long-term. Plan the year's topics and related images in advance on your editorial calendar.

Your Digital Magazine

A digital magazine is simply a PDF with text and images, formatted to look like a magazine. Because they are usually colorful, bold, and attractive, with catchy headlines and interesting text-wrap inside, people are drawn to them. They have a very high perceived value, and are the perfect medium for niche content, so it is quite easy to use them to attract your most ideal audience.

Your digital magazine can actually *be* your *Valuable Free Gift,* or it can be a stand-alone content piece you give your community as a special publication.

Creating and publishing a digital magazine can be time consuming and costly if you want it to be highly visual with lots of bells and whistles, many pages, and near perfect, yet it doesn't have to be. Sure, if you have the resources and the team, you can get your copywriter, graphic designer, and layout expert right on it, to produce a state-of-the-art digital magazine. Or, you can keep it simple (always my philosophy in life and business). Produce a digital magazine that's just twenty or so pages in length, with one amazing graphic (licensed, of course) per page or article. Select a captivating image and headline for the cover, and add some highlights of what's inside. You can hire a moderately-priced designer (try Elance.com) to do a decent layout using special magazine layout software, or create your pages in a program as basic as Word and convert the document to a PDF.

For each issue, *you* will write the main article. Select about eight or ten influential leaders in related niches to contribute feature articles your list would be excited about and interested in reading. If you are a decorator who specializes in window treatments for example, you would write the main article directly related to your expertise, then feature expert articles that support your brand and niche. Some suggestions might be articles on color psychology, furniture arranging, focal points, and having an organized home. All of these topics would appeal to your community without directly competing with you, while at the same time adding value to your brand.

BONUS TIP: There are many free programs online that will not only turn your Word document into a PDF, but host your magazine as well. All you have to do is sign up, upload your document, convert it, and share the link with your community and readers. It's like a miracle! Check out one such tool at **issuu.com**.

✓ **Publishing Frequency:** Publish your magazine two to four times annually. Plan the entire year in advance, including themes, topics, titles, images, and guest writers. Add this information to your editorial calendar.

Your Social Media

Social media is one communication channel that makes many people feel overwhelmed, and it's mostly because there are so many options. Again, I will go back to simplicity (it's best).

You clearly cannot be on all channels. So instead of doing a half-baked job of trying to show up as a leader on five or seven sites, show up strongly and consistently on one or two, then as you get proficient, or as your team grows, you can show up more frequently on more of them.

Your editorial calendar can help here. As you plan your blog posts and newsletter copy, you can pre-schedule social media posts that link to them, however, don't let those be your only social media transactions. The whole idea of social media is to be present in the moment. For your normal, regular, live interaction, select a few time slots during the day (scheduled) where you can invest a designated amount of time, and rock it!

Back in early 2010, I did one of my *Quickie Virtual Interviews* with author Seth Godin, and the advice he shared still applies today (and probably always will). He said, *"Pick a social media tool you love, and do it better than anyone else and ignore the rest."* I agree, although don't *completely* ignore the rest. Rather, show up strongly and consistently on one or two, and more occasionally on some of the others.

On your social media channels of choice, share inspirational messages and images that encourage and support others. In addition, work to build a community of individuals who see you as a thought leader and expert in your field who is helpful, personable, caring, and accessible. Allow plenty of time to build relationships. Think in terms of time investment.

Visuals are an important part of your influence on social media. Posts with images have a substantially increased incidence of engagement over posts without visuals (some experts say as much as ninety percent more). Choose images that relate well to your posts and that you have permission to use. If you want to really stand out with influence, create an infographic within your industry or niche that communicates data in a way that's easy to understand. A good infographic gets shared and passed around quickly. Be certain to include your web URL on the image. Another sharable visual you can create is a photo you own that's in line with your mission and brand, with an inspirational quote from *you,* and your URL.

Always provide value on social media. Be a positive and friendly resource, and absolutely stay clear of debates and negative interaction, like calling people out or correcting them publicly. You're safe when you do unto others as you would like them to do unto you. Yes, it's virtual, but it's all still *real*! Additionally, refrain from dumping business links or promoting your business outside of a clear context, and when you do post links, it should be only an occasional occurrence (no more than two out of ten posts).

Use social media as a relationship building tool. A great strategy for becoming an influential entrepreneur is to search social media sites for local people you would like to know (not sell to), and connect with them online. Be patient, as real relationships take time. Once the connection is there, take it further by meeting locally for lunch or coffee. I have created many strong and lasting friendships this way, and most of them have led to fantastic joint-venture projects.

✓ **Publishing Frequency:** Publish on two to three major social media sites daily (Facebook, LinkedIn, Twitter, Pinterest, Google +), once in the morning and once in the evening for each, when possible. Choose   the sites where your community members show up regularly. Use a combination of repurposed content that you reword, fresh content, and real-time inter-activity. Create some of the posts in advance, but only when appropriate, such as blog article links. Use scheduling software like HootSuite to automate occasional blog article sharing and more importantly, to manage social media.

Your Book

Write your book! As a content publisher and author, I write books. As a book publisher and content marketing consultant, I publish books through my company for professionals and business owners who want to become highly influential, and this I most certainly know: the single most significant thing you can do to appear as a notable expert is to author a book.

So start writing! Here's a super easy way to break the writing down: create a *working* (placeholder) title and tagline for your book (don't get stuck on the details), then make a list of twelve chapter topics (again, use *working* titles—no getting stuck on title details). Next, choose three *working* subtopics for each of the twelve chapters (these are your chapter headings). Now, choose one chapter per week, and write one heading on Monday, one on Wednesday, and one on Friday, filling the chapter in with a short introduction paragraph and a short conclusion paragraph for each chapter on the weekend. Best of all, you don't have to write the chapters in order! Instead, enjoy the freedom of writing each week on the chapter that tickles your fancy. In twelve weeks you will have written your entire book. Next proof it, format it, (preferably with professional editing and formatting) and publish it.

An alternative to a solo book is to co-author with one or two colleagues, or compile an anthology with a group. I help entrepreneurs do this all the time. It's the quickest way to author a book, and the most cost effective.

✓ **Publishing Frequency:** Publish one book in the next six to twelve months, and if you catch the fever, publish one book per year thereafter. That way, if you decide to publish only one book, you can at least call yourself a published author! Be sure to write on the topic for which you want to be known.

Brand publishing with engaging contents is a leadership choice! The entrepreneur who makes that choice is in for an exciting journey, and so are her clients! Through a solid content marketing plan you can connect, educate, and inspire, and position yourself for win-win engagement as an influential entrepreneur!

About Margo DeGange

Content Marketing & Publishing Expert, Margo DeGange, M.Ed., is an international best-selling author and speaker, and the founder of Women of Splendor, the exciting faith-based mentoring and networking organization where spiritually-minded entrepreneurs collaborate to become wildly successful. Quarterly, Margo hosts the life-transforming 4-Seasons of Success conferences.

Margo founded Splendor Publishing to help experts become published authors quickly and with ease, and bring their life-changing messages to others.

Known for business and lifestyle re-design, Margo can help you discover your authentic "Gift of Brilliance," then shine full throttle through content marketing from the heart!

Contact Margo at Margo@MargoDeGange.com

Learn More Here:
MargoDeGange.com *and* **WomenOfSplendor.com**

Continue the Conversation on . . .

Facebook: Facebook.com/Margo.DeGange
Facebook: Facebook.com/WomenOfSplendor
Twitter: Twitter.com/MargoDeGange
Twitter: Twitter.com/WomenofSplendor
Pinterest: Pinterest.com/MargoDeGange
LinkedIn: Linkedin.com/in/MargoDeGange

Chapter 7

Position, Engage, and Influence Your Way to a Healthy Business
by Michelle Brown Stephenson

Hello my friend, I am so very glad you have decided to meet me here. So you are ready to be a person of influence. You perceive there is a greater purpose for your life; you feel there is more to this existence than just paying bills and acquiring material things. Well come on in, the water is fine!

You are ready and willing to take the next step and I want you to know I'm very proud of you. You won't be disappointed in the outcome. Yes, it's a journey; but the fun, mystery, and intrigue will be well worth the effort. Let's jump right in and get you moving closer toward the finish line.

Healthy Positioning

Let's come to some common ground we can both agree upon—you must become comfortable with who you are. Do not compare yourself to anyone else. I know from firsthand experience; when you look in the mirror you see all of the flaws that are invisible to everyone else. You are unique, you were created that way. There's not another person quite like you. *You are an individual*. Okay, now that we have an understanding, just be yourself. You do what you were designed to do and you do it well.

Your next thought may be, *"How do I get my business in front of the people who need/want what I have a passion and expertise in?"* What are some common staples of your trade? Think a little harder and dig a little deeper into the well known facts society accepts as truths. Here's an example as it pertains to the healthcare industry: health care is major concern for many people. There is a lot of medical research and jargon in the media today. Most often than not, the general consumer is left feeling confused and overwhelmed. Yet current research shows that most people are looking for ways to feel young, vibrant, and energetic. So if these are the common truths in the minds of the people who need/want my passion and expertise, my goal is to ensure that these "common truths" are no longer an issue for my individual clients. This definitely positions our interactions together as valuable, meaningful, and important.

Allow me to provide you an example of how to position yourself using the healthcare example I used. Since I am a Public Health Educator, I had to really learn how to position myself as an expert on a variety of health issues. I had to be able to provide tangible, evidence-based health information that the client could understand. Positioning is being able to show your target audience that you have the expertise to give clear, concise health information that is evidence-based and has proven results. As the expert, your goal is to listen to the client and demystify the jargon, as well as define and simplify the medical research. To position yourself more effectively you must know your market. It is not enough to have passion— you must have knowledge of what they want, where they go, and their current needs. Information is ever changing, so keep up to date on the latest proven strategies in your field. Translating this information is key. People are individuals, so not everyone will take the same path to get to the ultimate goal. That touches on a big mistake many entrepreneurs make: if you try and apply one method to everyone in your target audience, you will jeopardize how you are positioned in the market. Explain things in terms familiar to the person you are speaking with. A teacher may prefer linear thoughts and processes while a carpenter may want to understand how systems fit together to make up the whole. The goal is still for the person to understand, but the journey taken and the mode of transportation must be customized.

One of the biggest lessons I have learned while discovering how to position myself in my market is to never look at the surface. Here is what I mean. When you actually analyze what your target audience wants and needs, the "real" issue is generally not on the surface. You will learn to make a conscious effort to listen and listen effectively. A person can just about hit the nail on the head when you listen for insight into how you can assist them. Because this is your field of business and your passion, please do not take it personally when the true value of what you offer is not fully comprehended. In my field, most people want to be well, and their definition of health is being without a known disease. However, people consistently suffer with unnecessary symptoms just because they do not understand the risk factors and how to tip the scale in their favor. In understanding my market, I learned how to master asking the right questions to discern or ascertain what they need while it may not always seem visible.

A positioning strategy that has been a gold standard in health education teaches you to meet the client where they are currently. You cannot fully facilitate sustainable behavior modification until you walk with the client in their shoes. A person will not incorporate a lifestyle change without the change being totally adaptable to their current situation. Remember you are an individual, and so are the clients you consult with. Case in point: different types of hair respond to the same product differently. Look at what you offer as a product or service. Then, examine how you approach or position your products and service. Next, determine how your client responds to you and how you have positioned yourself in the market. If you are not getting the response you want, ask yourself how you are positioned to your market? Are you listening to their needs? Are you addressing their wants?

Healthy Engagement

First things first—*listening is the key*. What happens so often with entrepreneurs is that in our effort to serve our audiences, we tend to regurgitate all we have, all we know, and all we are onto the potential client, and possibly on the first encounter. They then leave unfilled and totally confused. Can you relate? You must develop and learn to ask open-ended questions (no more than three or four) that will calm the client and allow them the time and medium to tell you what they want and need. For instance, if your niche is health education and you notice the client has a stuffy nose and red swollen eyes. Ask them to tell you what's going on and how long they have had these symptoms. If they mention it's a recurrent issue, ask what their routine is to get rid of these symptoms, or maybe ask what they think seems to cause the symptoms to flare up?

When you are attentive and take good notes, you will come up with a variety of items (short term and long term) you can assist that person in rectifying. Listening is an art, and it can be done effectively. Where is that person in their thought process? Do they know what they want, or do they need some direction? Are these symptoms recurring, and do they know why? Do they realize for every action there is a reaction or consequence?

Secondly, customer satisfaction is what builds good, productive connections. When a person feels you care and genuinely want to assist them in getting better, they open up and tell you exactly what they desire as a reasonable or acceptable outcome. Your ultimate goal should be to ensure you give them what they are looking for or toward. News flash: sometimes what they want may not be realistic, but they have to come to that understanding. As a health education specialist, when a person lacks the knowledge of how all the body systems work in conjunction with one another, you must coach/facilitate learning.

Thirdly, you must learn to prioritize the client's desires into a workable timetable. Start with the small details that will be able to be noticed in the least amount of time. This will enable to client to see results and feel accomplishment. Those red swollen eyes and stuffy nose could be signs of an allergy. You can make some general observations and make a few recommendations based on the answers given to your three or four questions. When the client is reaping benefits (relief from symptoms), a connection is made and satisfaction is realized.

Finally, ensure there is some way of following up with the client for support if they need re-assurance or just an outlet in which they can ask questions and receive answers. Not all people need this but for those who do, it is a life-line. If the client chooses, you can now begin to work through the other items they prioritized as desires to become reality. Some clients are ready for change and others just want to sample the "sweets on the platter." In time, you will be able to distinguish between the two. In my mind, motivation is the difference between staying the same and change. Why am I motivated to change my behavior? The person has been enduring a stuffy nose and red swollen eyes for years. If their mindset regarding these symptoms is that the symptoms are bearable or even something that *must be* forever, then change may not be their goal. When you follow up, ask if they have done the work to alleviate the symptoms. If they haven't, inquire tactfully as to why not? The answer will clue you in to whether or not they are motivated to change. There is always a reason that motivates change. Don't take it personally if change is not in their present mindset.

Do not get caught up in trying to *make* people see it the way you see it. There are many ways to get to the end goal, so let them find the path they want to choose to get to the final destination. Remember, this is a journey and the travel is part of the fun. Time has a way of bringing those who are ready to the understanding that they desire to change. You are passionate about what you do and your sincerity will be rewarded.

Healthy Influence

To start, I think this is where we need to define what is meant by influence. When I looked for definitions given for influence on the Internet, this is what I found:

Effect, impact, power, authority, sway, prestige, leverage, pull, stature, rank. -Oxford American Writer's Thesaurus Third Edition, and OxfordDictionaries.com

The capacity to have an effect on the character, development, or behavior of someone or something, or the effect itself. -OxfordDictionaries.com

The power to shape policy or ensure favorable treatment from someone, esp. through status, contacts, or wealth. -OxfordDictionaries.com

Now here is my definition of what influence is not. It's not your degrees on the wall, or being an expert in your field of business. It is not your name in lights, or money, or fame.

Influence is being known as the person to go to when results/answers are needed. If you are known for health answers in all of your circles (church, home, work, women's group), *that* is influence. If people tell others about what the issue or problem was and how your recommendation was the pivotal point that changed their situation, that's influence. It's how people remember you and what they say about you long after you are gone. It is the way you treat people every time just because you want to. Influence is the greater purpose you have in life, the reason you wake up every morning, and the gift you bring to the world at large. Everyone has a purpose, but only a few are actually living up to their purpose.

Genuinely, live to fulfill your purpose, your passion. The sun rises and sets on the way you choose to assist others. In other words, it starts and ends in your court. You set the tone of how you wish to influence the known market. When you give your very best, you gain personal fulfillment. Consistency in providing your product or service will build a solid foundation of trust and mutual respect with every client. Your reputation is built upon integrity—customer service.

Does the benefit the client receives enrich their lives? Does doing business with you feel like a gain or a loss? Do you rush through a presentation just to get the sale? Does the client truly understand why and how to utilize your product or service? Can the client articulate what they lose by choosing not to engage in business with you?

In conclusion, here is a brief "picture" of influence:

- Committed to living out your purpose with passion

- Relationships are built on mutual trust

- Credibility sprouts from benefits/gain being realized

- Relevance to the individual concerns, follow up

- Lives are changed for generations to come

Actionable Items

Positioning—Physically and Intellectually:

1. Develop and be comfortable with who you are and what you do.

2. Model in real time what you do to the persons that need/want what you have to offer. Evaluate whether you are effectively modeling your expertise to your clients.

3. Meet the client where they are and listen effectively to grasp a concept of reality for them.

Engagement—Availability and Accessibility:

1. Listen with the client in mind. Ask open-ended questions to gain clarity and insight. Ask at least three to five clients today, questions that will allow you to

deepen your relationship with them. This will help you serve them better and lengthen your client relationship.

2. Seek customer driven satisfaction—prioritize clients' desires into a workable timeline. When was the last time you surveyed your clients to ensure they are happy with what they are gaining from working with you?

3. Support and follow up with clients (Q&A, lifeline for change—if needed).

Caveat: Don't push. Allow them to journey in their own mode of transportation.

Influence—Legacy and Sustainability:

1. It's not how you perceive yourself, it's how others receive you—how are you remembered? **It's earned**!

2. Consistency (in integrity and customer satisfaction) influences the market place.

Note: Trust is built. Time is the environment in which it grows best.

3. Live to fulfill your purpose with passion (win/win situation—the client benefits and you are fulfilled).

About Michelle Brown Stephenson

Simply known as "The Nurse," Michelle Brown Stephenson is a knowledgeable professional with years of practical experience who provides valuable insight and interpretive guidance to help organizations, associations, and individuals navigate through the maze of the available health care options. She takes the time to help you understand your health concerns by de-mystifying the medical jargon. Michelle provides evidence-based, proven modalities and treatments that allow you to be an active participant on your healthcare team.

Learn More Here:
HealthOa.org

Continue the Conversation on . . .

Facebook: Facebook.com/michelle.brownstephenson.1
Twitter: Twitter.com/healthoa1
LinkedIn: Linkedin.com/in/healthoa

Chapter 8

From Purpose, Passion, or Patience Driven to "Influentially Driven"
by Crystal Jackson

"*Mom, one day I will travel the world and tell my story with an intent to motivate other teen mothers not to give up*," said Crystal L Jackson in the fall of 1998.

Unknowingly, at age twenty-three, I had identified my "purpose." However, it would be years later before I began to fully walk in that purpose. The announcement to my mother in the fall of 1998 may have been a great idea if considering a career in communications, but as a junior majoring in Computer Engineering this announcement seemed a bit odd to even myself. However, I knew within my heart I had a story teen mothers needed to hear.

At the mere age of sixteen, I found myself in a difficult situation. At the end of my sophomore year in high school I became pregnant, and gave birth the following fall of my junior year. Prior to my pregnancy, I would have been labeled as a student "*Most Likely to Succeed.*" However, statistics would now reveal a different truth in that more than fifty percent of teen mothers would never graduate high school, less than two percent would complete college by the age of thirty, and less than one percent of African American women graduate with Engineering degrees. With that being said, there was a story to be told.

It would be during this phase of my journey (before understanding what it meant to be an Entrepreneur) that I was driven solely by my "purpose." I had confessed with my mouth that I would become a speaker, however, it would be years later before I understood how to make it a reality.

Are you stuck in the "Purpose Driven" phase on your journey to becoming an influential entrepreneur? Do you believe in your business and services rendered, but find yourself stuck on purpose, prohibiting the growth of your business? If so, continue to journey with me through this chapter as I share tips to help you get unstuck.

"Passion" Driven

Approximately four years after verbalizing I would one day travel the world as a speaker, I secured my first "unpaid" speaking engagement.

On a beautiful spring day, I traveled back to my hometown of Muskogee, Oklahoma for my first speaking engagement at the local alternative high school. The students enrolled at this school had either been sent there from the public school or had opted to attend for various reasons. Many teen mothers ended up at the alternative school, so the choice to tell *"My Story"* at this particular school was not by accident. For two consecutive years I traveled back to speak a few times a year. During this time my "passion" for telling my story allowed me to impact the students in a very special way. Over time and with parents' permission, the school allowed me to adopt a special day. This special day was a way for me to show the young ladies I was committed to making a difference and that regardless of our circumstance we all have the capacity to become who we want to be. I coined the day *"Girls Day Out,"* and challenged the young women enrolled at the school to push past their limits and set goals of completing high school, while also considering higher education.

During this phase of my journey, I realized I had a story to tell that would be beneficial to the world, not just teen mothers. I had journeyed from "Purpose Driven" to "Passion Driven." Although my purpose and passion would keep the fire burning along my entrepreneur journey, I had yet to understand what it truly meant to become an entrepreneur or that I needed this thing called "influence" that would help connect me with my target market. My passion alone would not be enough to help me connect with the individuals who had the authority to book me as a "paid" speaker. So, I continued to speak at the alternative school and youth programs at various churches, and one hundred percent of the time it was for *free*.

Are you stuck in the "Passion Driven" phase on your journey to becoming an influential entrepreneur? Unsure? Answer the following question. Do you believe in your services so much that you are willing to give them away for *free*? If you answered "*Yes*," you are most likely stuck in this phase and will struggle to grow into an influential entrepreneur. However, don't fret. I am a few paragraphs from sharing tips for getting unstuck.

"Patience" Driven

Seven years after my last speaking engagement at the alternative school, I found myself back in my hometown but this time at a public school. I would continue to tell my story, however this time it was more impactful. Life had taught me valuable lessons as a teen mother, successful engineer, and now budding entrepreneur (or so I thought). This time around I had a website and business cards to prove I was a speaker. (Note: seek professional guidance when establishing a true brand.) To this day I chuckle at my first website created by yours truly. Lesson learned, I cannot be the speaker, assistant, website developer, and marketing expert. I wonder if that had anything to do with my "unpaid" speaking engagements.

I often look back and wondering how I kept the passion for speaking during my seven year hiatus, and I realized that I had transitioned from my "Passion Driven" phase to "Patience Driven." During my "Patience Driven" stage I grew as a career woman, in addition to an entrepreneur. It would be during this phase that I excelled as a leading African American engineer when less than one percent of the engineering population is comprised of African American women. It would also be during this phase of my journey that I realized I started to create a "brand." I allowed myself to grow as a woman, which created a better understanding of how to convey my message in a way to reach more than teen mothers.

Finally! Thirteen years after my initial announcement to my mother that I would one day travel the world and speak, I received compensation as a "professional speaker." Thirteen, yes, *thirteen* years from "unpaid" to "paid" and having an organization that is sweeping the country with its message and movement.

So, what changed? How did a little sixteen year old teen mother from a small country town create such a huge impact in her market space? Although *purpose, passion,* and *patience* were the key factors in staying the course and not giving up on my dream, those were not enough to create influence in my market space. Knowing my "purpose" was indeed a gift in itself, however, that alone was not enough. I had yet to create a true brand and identity for my target market. I had yet to create influence in a market that would connect me with my target audience and the platform that would allow me to tell "*My Story*" as a professional speaker.

Again I ask, what changed? I will tell you. Having a "no quit" attitude, investing in my growth, conveying my message in a way that allowed me to connect with my target audience, understanding my market, understanding my potential client's needs, and understanding the mindset behind influence and what was needed to grow to the next level.

I mentioned while in my "Passion Driven" phase I traveled back to my hometown for "unpaid" speaking engagements. When I first started out all I had was a dream; I had no blueprint of how I would ever become a speaker, and I am sure that was evident as you read through my *Purpose*, *Passion*, and *Patience* phases. So, I found myself trying to operate as a speaker with no mentor, and no business structure or business coach. *Purpose*, *Passion*, and *Patience* simply kept my dream alive.

What changed? How did I move from the "Patience Driven" phase? Well, the wait is over. I will answer those questions as you continue to journey with me. In the next section, I will provide tips that will help you avoid the delay in growing your business as revealed in my *Purpose*, *Passion*, and *Patience Driven* phases. These tips are created to help you avoid some of the pitfalls I encountered early on while evolving into an influential entrepreneur.

"Influentially" Driven

The saying "*You live and learn*" is a truth demonstrated in my business daily. Without going into the details of my business, I will say that every story, keynote presentation, workshop, seminar, etc. is a message from something life has taught me. On my journey to becoming an influential entrepreneur, experience taught me what *not* to do if I had the chance of going back to the "Purpose Driven" phase of my life. So, for the remainder of this chapter I will share with you three key tips to help you on your journey to becoming an influential entrepreneur.

Tip #1:
Understanding the "*Why*" Behind Your Business

When in doubt always ask "*Why*." You started your business ten years ago. Why? Do you have a heart for the services you are providing? If not, the target market you are trying to influence will know, as it will be difficult connecting with you as a person and brand.

Looking at my journey from the time I announced I would travel the world as a speaker to finally establishing a solid brand, it took over thirteen years. Why? It took thirteen years, not because I couldn't answer my "Why," but because I could not covey my "Why" in a way that connected with my target audience. Your "Why" is typically conveyed in the form of your *mission statement*, but it is more than making up a mission statement. Do you have passion for what it is you are selling? Do you believe in what you are selling? Would you buy what you are selling? If you answered "*Yes*" with your mouth, but "*No*" with your heart, you will most likely stay in your "Patience Driven" phase for a long time, never moving into your "Influentially Driven" phase. As entrepreneurs, we want to be successful and profitable, but at what cost?

I announced to my mother that I would become a speaker because in my heart I knew I had something to give others that would help make a positive impact in their lives. I had yet to understand how I would convey my message in a way to create influence, but I knew the "Why" behind my business long before setting up a business structure and long before compensation (today is a different day as it relates to compensation). Although I could not articulate my mission in a way to help create influence, I knew I wanted to help others push past obstacles.

Today, I can clearly articulate my mission *"To help individuals realize and fully maximize their potential by providing a platform for personal and professional growth."* That's my mission, but why do I want to *"help individuals realize their full potential"?* Because I believe all individuals have the power within to create their own success regardless of their circumstances. "Why" . . . why do I believe that? Because I beat incredible odds as a teen mother who graduated high school with honors and obtained scholarships to college when fifty percent of teen mothers will never graduate high school.

Today, I am an engineering leader at a large company and hold a Masters of Science degree in Systems Engineering, a Bachelor of Science degree in Computer Engineering, and a minor in Mathematics, while African American women make up only one percent of the engineering workforce. I am a recipient of the 2011 Black Engineer of the Year (BEYA) Modern Day Technology Leadership Award; a 1998 alumnus of The Washington Center, a leadership internship program in Washington DC; a published author; and founder of "The No Quit Zone."

So, I knew I had a story that must be told when my only accomplishment was graduating high school as a teen mother. However, knowing I had a story to tell was not enough. Seeking professional coaching that taught me "How" to tell my "Why" helped position my business to create influence.

That is my story . . . that is my "Why. " That is my purpose and I am sticking to it! What's the "Why" behind your business? Write your "Why" first on the tablet of your heart, then on your business tablet.

Tip #2:
Understanding the *"What"* Behind Your Brand

What does your brand say about you? What message are you conveying to your target market? Are you trustworthy? Do you believe in what you are selling? Do you deliver as promised? Are you relatable?

One of my favorite quotes by Oprah Winfrey is *"Your life is speaking to you, what is it saying?"* Take a minute to think about it. Your life is speaking to you, what is it saying? The same holds true for your brand. *"Your brand is speaking to you, what is it saying?"*

Your brand is a reflection of yourself. From as early as four years old, I can recall being a talker and very curious. I was definitely a conservationist, so much so that my nickname became "motor mouth" as a small child. At the mere age of four years old my life was speaking to me. Since I can remember I was a communicator, so my announcement in 1998 to my mother was in alignment with the message my life had been conveying. However, at age four I hadn't lived enough to tell my story in a way that would impact the world.

However, they say with age comes wisdom. Well, little motor mouth never lost her passion to speak and be heard. During my *Passion* and *Purpose* stages of my life, all I wanted to do was tell *"My Story."* I hadn't put much thought into the packaging. I showed up to my engagements and spoke from the heart. However, from the beginning I have always had a very unique way of telling my story. I consider myself a "Journey Teller." Rather in the form of writing or on stage in front of thousands, I have a way of creating a story and image that creates a connection with my audience, which allows them to feel as though they are journeying with me.

In my early stages as a speaker, I hadn't placed much thought into establishing a brand, yet to my surprise, my gift of communication coupled with self-confidence, hard work, problem solving, and motivating, *was* my brand. I started to pay attention to the feedback received from speaking engagements or encounters with others who were moved by my message. "*Motivating*," "*Inspirational*," "*Confident*," *Hard-Working*," "*Trustworthy*," "*Problem Solver*" . . . those were the consistent qualities that resonated with others.

The qualities that resonated with others were a reflection of what my life spoke about me. However, it would be years later—in my first business coaching session—that I established a true brand. The phrase "No Quit Zone" was created while working with a professional marketing and branding coach, since I had been conveying the "No Quit" attitude in my everyday life and message. With the help of a professional business coach, I realized my life was telling a story and the consistent message was "*Do not quit!*" Also, the "how" behind my message was consistently being recognized in the qualities others would identify in me.

Had I known then what I know now, I would have sought a professional marketing and branding/business coach years ago. I later realized that was the difference between an "unpaid" and "paid" speaking engagement. Coaching helped me to really understand the message I was trying to convey and how to package it in a way that would effectively reach my target market. The day I launched my new website for the "No Quit Zone," with Crystal L Jackson as the "No Quit Speaker," was the day I booked my first "paid" speaking engagement as a "professional speaker."

What changed? My message was the same and my key characteristics were the same. Now, my business packaging was different. I had established a true brand that allowed me to convey my message in a way that connected with the organizations that would later book me. I had a new website, professional pictures that mirrored my confidence, clear and concise speaking topics, and a mission statement written on the tablet of my heart.

Your brand is speaking to you, what is it saying?

Take Action

✓ Write five key strengths of your brand.

✓ Write five areas of improvement needed for your brand.

✓ Write an action plan for transiting "areas of improvements" to "strengths" in your business.

Tip 3:
Understanding the "*How*" Behind Growing Your Business

Understanding the "Why" behind your business and being able to convey it in a way that connects with your target market is the first order of business. Understanding the "What" behind your brand and the message your brand is conveying is the second order of business.

After understanding the "Why" and "What" behind your business and brand, you are ready for the "How." How can you leverage understanding the "Why" and "What" to grow your business to the next level?

I mentioned that after seeking professional coaching and creating the "No Quit Zone" brand, I secured my first "paid" speaking engagement. I failed to mention, though, that as a "professional speaker," video footage is critical to creating influence in my market space and securing bookings. Well, I failed to have that critical marketing piece as a speaker. Prior to establishing a true brand, I barely had a website, so my taped video footage was way past poor. However, because I now had a true brand, a mission statement that I was able to clearly articulate, confidence, high energy, and a way of immediately establishing a connection with my potential client, I secured most bookings from face-to-face communication rather than video footage. As an influential entrepreneur (professional speaker), my mission is to "help individuals realize and fully maximize their potential by providing a platform for personal and professional growth" (the "Why"). I provide fun, high-energy, engaging programs that are articulated with confidence through different forms of communication (the "What").

Being able to articulate the "Why" and understanding the "What" is not enough to grow your business. Packaging is a key element to growth as well. Do you have a website that connects you with your target market? Does your website align with your brand? Does your marketing material align with your brand? Are you extending your influence into all entry points of your business? When given the opportunity to connect with a potential client, can you convey your *mission* (the "Why") in a way that creates interest? Does your brand (the "What") then help secure the deal? If not, I challenge you to revisit the total packaging of your business. If you cannot articulate the mission of your business in a way that draws interest and has the potential to create influence, you will most likely struggle with growing your business to the next level. If your brand is not represented in a way that connects you to your target market, I challenge you to revisit your total business packaging. Are you packaged for growth?

Take Action

✓ Do your marketing products represent your brand (website, photos, newsletters)?

✓ Is your marketing campaign creating influence?

The simple truth I mentioned at the beginning of this section, "*You live and you learn*" is only true when one is open to learning. If I had known then what I know now, understanding these three simple tips would have been the difference between an "unpaid" and "paid" speaking engagement.

If you consider yourself stuck in the *Purpose, Passion,* or *Patience Driven* phases of your business, with a desire to move into the *Influentially Driven* phase, I challenge you to use these tips to get "unstuck" on your journey to become an influential entrepreneur.

About Crystal Jackson

Crystal L. Jackson is a professional development speaker and trainer, or better known to others as the *"No Quit Speaker."* Crystal is passionate about connecting with women and inspiring them to maximize their full potential. Crystal's extraordinary ability to connect with women and present real information with no fluff or smoke & mirrors will help the everyday woman shift from an *"I Can't"* to an *"I Can"* mindset by providing a blueprint for personal and professional growth.

Learn More Here:
CrystalJackson.org

Continue the Conversation on . . .

Facebook: Facebook.com/thenoquitzone
Twitter: Twitter.com/c_l_jackson

Chapter 9

Position Yourself for
Work-Optional Wealth!
by Judi Snyder

What is "Work-Optional Wealth?" Simply stated, it is wealth that makes work "optional." This is a simple concept but difficult to achieve . . . maybe not. If we can learn three powerful lessons early enough in our career, work-optional wealth can be yours long before the government sanctioned "retirement" age of 59.5 years old!

It took me till my late forties to learn these lessons. I wish I had learned them in my twenties. For this reason, I've become passionate about sharing these lessons with investors of all ages. Why is my passion around money, specifically investments? If you can create wealth that makes work optional, you have the freedom to pursue your passions without compromising your values for a paycheck.

Although I had a very successful track record of making money, I had **no idea** about investing and making money for *me* . . . I made lots of money for companies, but when it came to my personal investments, I let others do the "thinking" for me. The delegation of such an important area of my life was totally out of character for me. I'm a "Type A" personality, which is an individual who is characterized as ambitious, highly competitive, and who generally needs to feel "in control." This would certainly apply to making major decisions, particularly important ones such as those related to my money. Yet here I was handing over all of my overachiever compensation to people I didn't know, to put it in strategies I knew nothing about, with companies I knew nothing about, for an unknown period of time, and a return that no one could begin to predict and or guarantee. WOW . . . talk about incongruence.

I was considered a pretty savvy businessperson with an above average knowledge of money. I grew up with a very successful entrepreneur father and worked by his side from the age of eleven until I graduated from college. I studied Psychology and Business Management in college and was pleasantly surprised to learn that there were actually volumes of books written, and curriculum, on the very work I did with my father since I was eleven. I had eight years of management experience by the time I sat in my first business class.

You would think that with all of my privileged education and early work experience with a father who had the "Midas Touch" in business, I would understand investments. I didn't. Like with many of us, money wasn't really discussed at the dinner table. There is a huge disconnect between our comfort level with *making* money, and *investing* money. We are comfortable "making money" because we do this 250 days or more a year. However, when it comes to "making investment decisions" we probably spend less than one day a year on those decisions.

I Didn't Know There was a Difference Between Making and Keeping Money

The difference between money psychology and investing psychology occurred serendipitously to me one day while having a conversation with my cousin. We were discussing investment decisions. The discussion centered around the statement *"people only make a change with their investments for one of three reasons: fear, greed, or disgust."* The prickly words generated an instant visceral reaction from my cousin. He replied *"I love money, I love making money. I don't believe I have any of those emotions around making money."* He was right, he had worked on his relationship with money so successfully that he had the ability to make money with joy.

Here comes my "Aha" moment . . . my response was, *"I'm not talking about **making** money, I am talking about **investing** money. Do you still have the same joyful energy and positive emotion around investing?* Guess what? His answer was a resounding *"No"*! Investing money was another story. He had his own epiphany when he realized the disparate feelings between making and investing money. How could this little piece of green paper evoke positive emotions when earning it and "darker" emotions when investing it?

There are some fundamental things we must know before we invest a dime. Beginning with these steps will allow you to put mindful investing on autopilot so you are free to focus on your gifts and passion.

Know Your "Number"—Cash Flow is Royalty! *(My husband and I disagree on which one is most important, Queen or King!)*

Before we can begin the details of "work-optional wealth" we must first understand our baseline or starting point. We must first define the "purpose" of our money. Most people have a common purpose for their money; which is to support them until they pass away. Now, there may be other purposes, but for the majority of the population, some of their savings will   be used to support their lifestyle through retirement. In order to develop a plan that will use a portion or perhaps all of your money to support you in later years, we must first understand our "number."

We start by determining the amount of money you need to have on an annual (or monthly) basis to cover your living expenses. In essence, what does it cost to fund your lifestyle? This is the minimum amount of money you need to generate through investment interest or work to be able to fund your lifestyle *stress free!*

We will look at our expenses in three areas:

- Current income needs

- Future income needs

- Gaps in either area

Current

Start determining how much money you will need by figuring out what your baseline is at this very moment with your current obligations. Current obligations may include mortgages, taxes, insurances, car payments, home expenses, children's expenses such as education, car, health, and other general expenses.

Future

When defining future, include all the remaining years of your mortgage, equity loans, property taxes, and insurances. You will also want to include any anticipated expenses such as children going to college, new car every five to seven years, etc.

If you don't know how much income you need or will need, it will not be possible to accurately plan for your future, either pre-59.5 or post 59.5. I use 59.5 as a gauge because that's the age when you can access qualified accounts (IRA, 401K, 403B, Roth IRA) without penalty.

Gaps

Gaps may include health insurance; both medical and long-term care insurance. It may also be the difference between your wages or earnings, and "retirement" social security payments, or having three children in college at the same time. The gaps will most likely be different for everyone. It is very important to know your gaps well in advance, so you can plan for them accordingly. By having this knowledge at your fingertips, you can work with a good financial planner to address the gaps and put a plan in place to meet your needs for the future.

Decide How Much Liquidity You Need to be Comfortable

You must decide how much liquidity you need to keep your investments. It is imperative that you seriously consider any possibility of needing your money so you do not end up badly needing funds that are tied up for a long-term hold. Decide how much money you can invest for different time horizons. Some examples of time horizons include:

- Immediate

- Short-term (within the next two years)

- Mid-term (within the next two to five years)

- Long-term (five or more years)

Only invest monies that you do not need for cash flow or other needs. It is always advisable to have a safe emergency fund that is easily accessible. Your advisor can make suitable recommendations for your situation. I believe the best formula is whatever allows *you* to sleep at night! It is you not an advisor who must decide what truly allows you "Sleep Equity" or the ability to sleep at night!

Sources of liquidity should be layered and have a hierarchy for withdrawal. In other words, you should have a number of sources of potential liquidity and a predetermined sequence for accessing those sources. For example, you may have a checking account, a savings or money market account, a certificate of deposit, an annuity, a line of credit on real estate, and a cash value life insurance policy with a loan provision. When you need funds, where do you go first? A general rule of thumb would be to go to the lowest cost, lowest yielding investment first. In this example, you would go to the checking account, followed by the savings account.

What is the right target level for these liquid accounts? The answer is always the same: it depends. There are emotional and financial factors that play into what's right for you. How much liquidity do you need to sleep at night? What is the maximum amount of liquidity you have ever needed in the past? How long would it take to reestablish your target liquidity amount? By thinking through these questions and building a multi-layered liquidity plan, you can arrive at your starting targets. You will then be able to adjust them over time based on your experience and changes in your circumstances.

Investing is a Process, *Not* a Destination

Just like the process for purchasing a cell phone or vacation package begins with knowing the amount of money you have budgeted to spend, so does the process of investing.

The process—or "Money Rules for Investing"—is a dynamic process that will change over time with age, income, investable assets, marital status, and market conditions. Take time annually to review your "Money Rules," and make the appropriate changes. Having money rules around your business, spending, savings, debt management, and investing will put your money on autopilot! Having money rules for dealing with family and friends can save your money, but most of all your cherished relationships.

Systematizing money rules by carefully considering these areas will help you determine a roadmap for successful investing help you develop a plan, without emotion or peer influence compromising your core values, goals, and objectives. Perhaps the most under discussed is "Investing Rules," yet how we approach investing has everything to do with our financial freedom day. Many of us don't know where to begin, so let's focus on the "moving parts" of an investment.

INVESTMENT RULES

Anatomy of an Investment

This is one of the most important areas of your financial health. Understanding the "moving parts" or components to an investment will help you to determine your own personal preferences for any investment, because all investments have the same components. Knowing where you feel most comfortable on each of those "moving parts" will become your "Money Rules for Investing!" Money rules do not guarantee that you will not experience losses in your investments, but they will guarantee that there will be very few surprises.

By understanding the heart and soul of an investment, you are able to make mindful choices without surprises. You can make decisions and seek out investment strategies that will preserve the money you need for your "number" and protect your vision.

Determine the Liquidity or Exit Event for Your Investment—Readily Available or Long-Term Hold?

Liquidity or exit event simply means, "when will I get my money back?" Never enter into any investment without the end in mind.

Choose Your Investment Objective: Cash Flow or Appreciation? (Current Cash Flow, Future Cash Flow, or Appreciation)

Decide what percentage of your portfolio you wish to allocate to generating current cash flow or future cash flow, and what percentage you wish to allocate to producing appreciation. This basically means money now or money later. This will heavily depend on your "number." Your "money now" should supplement your current cash flow needs. Your "money later" can be allocated in appreciation strategies, and that often has higher growth potential. You can also combine strategies to create a hybrid of current and future cash flow along with appreciation.

Decide How Much Participation You Want or Have Time for In Your Investments (Active, Passive, or Pactive)

Decide what percentage of your portfolio you wish to be active versus passive. Active means that you do the work. Passive means you don't. An example of a passive investment would be a "structured settlement" or a "fixed annuity." It is a "set it and forget it" strategy. In truth, most investments tend to have an element of both. Loral Langemeier coined the term "pactive" because when we "lead our wealth" we must always drive our investment portfolio and be involved on some level, but perhaps not day-to-day.

Understand Risk Approach (Accept, Manage, Avoid, or Transfer)

Does anyone really have tolerance when it comes to losing his or her money? I believe this characteristic of an investment is one of the least understood yet most critical to investment success. By truly understanding risk approach and how each of your investment choices operate, you are able to protect and grow your money without surprises. You begin leading your wealth and making more mindful choices. Your money begins working for you, not the other way around.

Ed Winslow, author of *Blind Faith*, outlined four ways of approaching any kind of risk. They are: ***Avoid***, ***Accept***, ***Manage*** or ***Transfer*** risk. Any investment you will ever consider approaches risk in one of these four ways.

Avoid Risk: Investment strategies that do not place your principal at risk and normally would offer some type of guaranteed return would be an example of avoiding risk. Some strategies would include CDs, savings accounts, or traditional fixed annuities. The "mattress" and "cookie jar" can also be risk avoidance.

Accept Risk: Investment strategies that place your principal at risk and do not offer any contractual guarantees, only the "potential" of high returns, such as the stock market. Stocks are called "securities" and are regulated by the Security Exchange Commission or the "SEC."

Manage Risk: Investment strategies that attempt to manage risk in an effort to minimize it, such as money managers, mutual funds, hedge funds, and even some Private Placement Memorandum or PPM's. One way to manage risk is to use a "money manager" who will attempt to minimize the risk with asset allocation and diversification.

Transferring Risk: Investment strategies that transfer the risk of loss of principal to experts in exchange for contractually guaranteed principal protection and participation in market gains. These strategies typically trade off a small portion of the potential upside to have **none** of the downside or potential loss during downturns or market declines. Some examples of these strategies are fixed annuities, fixed index annuities, structured settlements, and life settlements.

Other Risk Considerations

When determining what portion of your money you are willing to accept or manage risk, you also need to consider, are you a

W2 employee? Is your salary "at risk" money? Outside of the obvious illegal or non-performance reasons, you have no control over your company and their decision to terminate your employment. Companies move, go bankrupt, and products lose their allure, so consider this when determining how "safe" your paycheck money really is.

Whatever your decision, particularly if you have chosen to accept risk, have a risk management plan. If you aren't using a "money manager," seek out educational tools to help you put market signal alerts in place. There are many programs you can use to input your 401K or IRA funds and they will send you signal alerts when you should step to the sideline or change funds. They do a nice job of putting some control back to you and helping you to protect and safely grow your 401K and IRAs.

Aim for a Specific Target Rate of Return (Historical Rate of Return in "REAL" Numbers)

You can determine this by the Annualized Rate of Return or the Overall Return on Investment approach. You can set minimum limits and goals for each type of investment account, or you can simply set overall minimum limits and goals for all of your investments.

Target rate of return is the "interest" rate a specific investment is projected to return. This could be a compounded interest rate or a simple interest rate.

Know whether your investment is designed for simple interest or compound interest and understand the difference between the two.

Simple Interest Rate: Interest paid or computed on the original principal.

Compounded Interest Rate: Interest computed on the sum of an original principal and accrued interest.

Understand "Wall Street" math. Wall Street math will often throw percentage returns around such as market is up ten percent this year; market is up the last six months. But here is the ugly truth . . . If you lose fifty percent of $100,000 you need a one hundred percent return just to be at $100,000! Let's do the math:

$$\$100,000 - 50\% = \$50,000$$

Now if we have a percent return, how much money do we have?

$$\$50,000 + 50\% \text{ return} = \$75,000$$

That my friends is what no one is talking about and that is why most are just about even with the amount of money they had in the market in 1999 until today . . . all these years later and most are "just about even."

Whatever your choice, the important thing is that you know what you are trying to accomplish with each investment you make and that you have a reasonable expectation to accomplish your goal(s) with each investment. And remember, the standard cost of living increase is three percent. In other words, understand the purpose of your money and be realistic with the returns.

Know the Tax Ramifications of the Investments You Have and Those You are Thinking About (Tax Advantages or Consequences)

While you never want to make an investment decision solely based on taxes, you must consider the effects that your investments will have on taxes and regular income. Some investments will create returns that impact the taxes you pay on your ordinary income. A great year in your investments could mean that your regular income is taxed at a much higher rate. A horrible year in ordinary income may be a great time to convert to a "Roth" from a traditional IRA because your tax bracket may be lower. Many people pay AMT, or Alternative Minimum Tax, when there are strategies that may mitigate these taxes. An excellent strategy for mitigating your AMT tax bill is an investment in oil and gas wells, which will offset those taxes and yield returns for generations!

Hire the Expertise You Don't Have—Brain Trust or Team

Be sure part of your financial team includes a "tax strategist"— CPA, tax strategist, and/or tax attorney (recommended for significant wealth) to help you plan how to move your money in and out of investments over time to take full advantage of the tax code as it relates to investments. The tax strategists must be strategic and not "form fillers!"

Choose professionals who are more successful than you and whose clients include high net worth individuals and other successful business owners. Choose specialists, not generalists. You wouldn't go to an internist to get cardiac bypass surgery! When you work with a professional whose expertise is in specific areas, they will know all of the subtle nuances of the tax code and can optimize your tax situation.

Know Your Options in Each Asset Class

True diversification includes many different asset classes and will likely include strategies outside of traditional Wall Street offerings. If you limit yourself to a Wall Street-based portfolio, including stocks, bonds, mutual funds, and REITs (international, small caps, and mid caps), you are only diversifying within one asset class. If/when there is a systemic downturn, they are all likely to crash!

Have at least some of your money in asset allocation vehicles that are either uncorrelated to market conditions or have the protection of your principal safety built into the contract. Your model may only include two asset classes, and that is okay; just make sure they are based on your goals and objectives.

Some examples of various asset classes include:

- Securities (stocks, mutual funds, bonds, variable annuities, REITS, and other derivatives)

- Insurance and insurance-backed investments (life settlements, structured settlements, fixed indexed annuities, whole or universal life-banking on yourself concept)

- Real Estate

- Oil & Gas

- Forex

- Gold, silver, and precious metals

- Businesses/DPP (Direct Participation Programs)

- PPM (Private Placement Memorandum)

- Promissory notes

- Cash on hand

- Other (mortgage notes, collectibles, etc.)

By understanding all of the "moving parts" of an investment and including your personal values, goals, and objectives in your financial decisions, your portfolio becomes *your* investment portfolio and *not* the advisors portfolio, which is often based on the availability of offerings dictated by their company or license. Learning about investing can be a daunting task but a necessary task. Choose a financial team that is right for you.

Three Things I Wish I Knew

There are three things I wish I knew when I began making money. These three things are simple yet powerful lessons that will allow you to begin the path to your financial freedom day:

1. Passive residual income and compound interest is the "name of the game!"

2. The difference between investing and speculating

3. All advisors are biased . . . and they should be. But that means you must understand investments and seek the "best in class" professionals who represent your goals and objectives, not theirs.

1. Passive Residual Income and Compound Interest is the "name of the game!"

You must have the right goal to begin achieving work-optional wealth. For many of us we were taught to get a "job" with a financially stable company, climb the corporate ladder and work sixty-hour work-weeks with little time for vacation for thirty years with the same company and retire with a pension. That just doesn't exist anymore so you have to have a different goal. The new goal should be to create a passive residual income that has a high probability of compounding your investment returns. By creating multiple streams of passive residual income over time we can eventually stop trading time for money. Most would say that money gives you more freedom but that isn't entirely true. The other half of that equation is how much time it takes you to make the money and how much time you have to spend it. Even the highest-paid brain surgeon is trading time for money. Time is the ultimate form of wealth because everyone is born with the same twenty-four hours in a day and only fiscally smart people free more time for their desires.

Having enough money AND time allows us to pursue our passions and use our gifts and talents to make a bigger impact in the world. If we have the stress of paying mortgage and bills we erode our time and energy we could be spending on serving the world with our gifts.

Because we are taught that our most important ROI is "return on investment," we spend too many important years chasing returns and taking risks that lose our principle and perhaps our entire investment. I challenge the "traditional" definition of ROI and say the most important ROI is not always "return on investment" but rather "reliability of income." If you have reliable income plans for now and into the future it's going to do two important things. First, give you peace of mind or as we call it "sleep equity." Sleep equity allows you to sleep at night because you are not worried about your investments or your income.

Using "guaranteed" financial strategies to cover what it will cost to continue our lifestyle without hardship (our "lifestyle" needs), is paramount to an early financial freedom day. By using guaranteed strategies for our basic needs, knowing we can never lose our principle or gains, we free up the rest of our portfolio to take on more risk or achieve other goals such as long-term growth, legacy or charity.

2. The Difference Between Investing and Speculating

Another very powerful concept is the difference between an investment and speculation and whether or not compound interest is working for you or against you. Too often we have compound interest working against us because we are speculating and we don't understand investment mathematics.

Let's begin with the definition of investing or an investment. Investment is allocating our principle (or money) to a protected or guaranteed strategy in which our principle is protected and guaranteed and our gains are added to our original principle and we can never go backwards. Speculation is defined as taking a risk that our principle (or money) may make a return but may also lose the original principle or money allocated to the strategy. Most of us don't understand the mathematics of losses or the "flaw of averages."

Flaw of Averages

Earlier we talked about "Wall Street math." The reason that so many investors are flat from 1998 to 2014 even though the market averaged a seven to eight percent return during the same period of time is because we didn't harvest the returns when we received them. When we don't harvest the returns when we receive them, they evaporate with the volatility. Think of playing blackjack in a casino. If you start with one hundred dollars and you play until you are up seven hundred dollars, until you take your chips off the table and cash in, that money still belongs to the casino. The same holds true with the stock market. Until you harvest your gains that money still belongs to Wall Street.

Another part of investment mathematics that is little understood is the *"sequence of returns."* The "flaw of averages" combined with the timing of withdrawing our investment funds can and will affect our overall returns. There is a story about a man who can't swim and was told he had to cross the river immediately. He was scared because he couldn't swim but his companions quickly said *"don't worry, the river is only an average of five feet deep."* The problem is that it was two feet deep in some parts and twenty feet deep in other parts. So, if you can't swim, the fact that it's an average of five feet deep doesn't matter to you because you're still going to have to confront twenty feet deep waters.

Compounded interest can work against you as well, for example, debt. Not all debt is created equal. There is good debt and bad debt. Good debt would be a fixed interest rate on our primary residence or a fixed rate on a loan or line of credit for business expansion. Bad debt would be credit cards and loans used to finance lifestyle. If you only pay the minimums on credit card debt, the balance multiplies and it begins to spiral downward and can really set our financial freedom day back. Be sure to use compound interest for your benefit not your detriment.

Understanding our investment risk in each strategy, how investment mathematics will determine our potential gains and losses, and the sequence of returns when it is time to withdraw our money is key to building lasting wealth. This will have a huge impact on whether or not we will make money and when we will reach financial freedom day.

3. All Advisors are Biased

. . . and they should be. But that means we must understand the moving parts to our investments. This includes knowing which asset class that investment is a part of and seeking the "best in class" professional(s) who represent the respective asset class. A good advisor will include our personal goals and objectives, not theirs.

You want an investment advisor who knows their strategy inside and out—the best in class provider and expert in the field. However **a well-diversified portfolio should be diversified across asset classes** not diversified within one asset class. As we saw in 2008 when that asset class experienced a downturn, all of the investments—regardless how diversified they were—went down because they were all highly correlated to each other. All ships rise and fall with the tide when they are in the same body of water.

The more money we have to invest, the bigger our team of advisors needs to be. Choose advisors who believe in cooperative money, not competitive money. There will always be one advisor who acts as your "quarterback," but they should be willing to support your investments into asset classes they do not offer. In order to choose our team, we must seek enough education and information to determine the asset class(es) in which we want to invest, and then be able to identify the best in class advisers to provide that asset class.

We need to lead our wealth, and to lead our wealth we need to lead our team of advisors. **Leading our wealth protects our interests and helps us develop reasonable expectations for our portfolio.** Allowing our advisors to make recommendations and choices does not mean we don't do our "due diligence" (or research) when it comes time to invest our money. It is our responsibility to research the recommendations. The Internet has made this task both easy and difficult. Easy because there is a plethora of information at the push of a button, and difficult because anyone can say anything and it is often assumed true. Information stays on the Internet forever regardless of whether it is true or false. Check references and ask for sample portfolios. Be true to your principles and have a truly diversified portfolio across all asset classes. Mitigate volatility and be congruent with your personal goals.

Three Things You Can Do Right Now!

1. Determine your "number" so you will know how much money you need today, tomorrow, and to reach your "Financial Freedom Day." Knowing your number will help you determine how much money you can safely contribute to your wealth plan.

2. Develop your personal "investment money rules" so you can attract investments that serve *you*! Include diversification among asset classes and know which advisors offer the specific asset classes.

3. Commit to contributing a minimum amount of money into a strategy that protects your principle and has a guaranteed return, so you can begin compounding interest on your money and reach your "Financial Freedom Day" sooner rather than later!

About Judi Snyder

Judi Snyder is a partner at JP Snyder, Inc., a "boutique" investment firm. She is a Certified Financial Transitionist, CFT™ through The Sudden Money Institute, and Investment Coaching.

We are *"Experts in the Best Investments You've Never Heard of!"* Our proprietary approach specializes in "alternative financial strategies" uncorrelated to today's volatile stock market, declining real estate market, and political or economic conditions. We believe in a collaborative approach to investing and that every investor should have a team of advisors.

Since our inception in 1998, not one of our clients **ever** lost a dime in any single investment!

Learn More Here:
JPSnyder.com

Continue the Conversation on . . .

Facebook: Facebook.com/WealthOffWallStreet
Twitter: Twitter.com/wealthoffwallst
LinkedIn: Linkedin.com/in/judijosephsnyder

Chapter 10

BONUS
MENglish® and WOMENglish® Top Ten List
by Andrea C. Jones

"*How are you?*" is a common greeting here in the United States. "*I am fine, how are you?*" is the expected response. Think about this for a moment: how often have you said the above phrase within the last week? And now reflect on this: how often did you really care about the other person's response?

During my first visit to the United States over twenty years ago, I went into a shoe store. Upon entering, a female sales associate came over and asked me, "*How are you?*" I thought to myself, "*Wow, Americans are so nice!*" My English wasn't that great back then so it took me a few seconds to translate the answer in my head, and by the time I was ready to respond she was already with another customer. Today I would not think twice about her behavior, but back then I was baffled, and quite honestly, offended. I immediately judged the sales associate as being rude. Do not ask me a question if you do not care about my answer.

If you have ever been to Germany, you have experienced that Germans are not going to ask you "*How are you?*" because quite frankly, unless you are a family member or friend, we really do not care. In a store the question will be, "*How can I help you?*"

Going back to my story, the sales associate communicated in a way that is not only common here in the United States, but actually expected. Not asking, *"How are you?"* is considered out of the norm. However, she was speaking with a German who was raised in a different culture with a dissimilar communication style, and she achieved the opposite of what she had intended. I was turned off by her behavior and left the store without buying any shoes (and I love shoes).

What is so crucial about what I just shared is that as an entrepreneur, it's important for you to understand the clients you are trying to reach. Knowing how to treat potential clients and existing clients in a way that makes them feel like they are an audience of one is critical to your success. Are you approaching your potential clients and customers in a way that will cause them to engage with you? Are you customizing your approach in how you communicate with them, market to them, and work with them?

When I eventually moved to the United States, I had to learn to adapt to the American way, as certain German manners do not work well here. I faced a lot of obstacles I had to overcome. Learning about the American culture, the *dos and don'ts* in doing business with U.S. corporations, and dealing with American business professionals was the only way I could succeed. This adaptation did not mean I had to change who I was or give up my core values, it just meant that in order to be successful, I had to adjust my behavior and communication style.

Both culture and upbringing have a lot to do with how we communicate, especially how we communicate with each gender. I want you to be as effective as you can as an entrepreneur of influence, particularly in the area of gender communication. This is vitally important for you as a business owner who will undoubtedly deal with both men and women in various settings.

You may have heard the saying, *"Men are from Mars, and Women are from Venus"* (John Gray). Well, men and women have different "wiring," and in the same way we respond to each other differently in relationships and life in general, we do the same in business. Men and women handle business from a different approach. Of course, men and women are *equal*, but the reality is we simply do not want to be treated the same. We want to be understood!

In my work, I help individuals successfully communicate with both men and women in a way that's beneficial and empowering. Over the years, through my work and research, I have identified several key truths that if understood and applied, can help us relate better to each of the sexes, and open the door to greater connection. As a BONUS to this book, I have put together for you a *MENglish® and WOMENglish® Top Ten List* so you will have these keys close at hand and at-a-glance when you need them (and please keep in mind, the items listed here are generalities based on research and data, and do not necessarily specifically apply to everyone). I hope you enjoy them, and use them to create greater impact and engagement with others as you become an influential entrepreneur.

MENglish® and WOMENglish® Top Ten List

1. Most men consider it a strength (while women consider it a weakness) to be inexpressive, unemotional, and direct in their communication with others (so keep this in mind when communicating with men).

2. Most women consider it a strength (while men consider it a weakness) to give attention to and share details, as well as to show empathy toward others when they are communicating (so again, keep this in mind in your interactions with women).

3. When communicating with a man, stick to the facts and the basics without being "wordy." This helps you to be perceived as credible and competent, which builds trust and respect.

4. When communicating with a woman, you will build greater trust when you share information and details within a relative context, rather than sticking just to the basic facts.

5. In the sales process with a woman, don't make it about the "thing." She is not buying an item; she is buying the emotional benefits the item will provide her.

6. Keep in mind that women influence as much as eighty-five percent of all buying decisions (especially those related to the home or family). Consider this fact in terms of your marketing budget and activity.

7. When speaking with a woman about your products and services, bring the conversation back to how it will affect her family and/or lifestyle.

8. If you are a woman communicating with a man, allow space for moments of silence without becoming uncomfortable.

9. Often, both men and women know how they *should* behave, but deep-seated beliefs and cultural conditioning can drive behavior (and this behavior may not be the *best* or most ideal behavior).

10. As professionals and responsible adults, we must make it a point to become aware of our behavioral tendencies, and adapt our behavior to what is appropriate in each setting.

Most all of us believe in gender equality, but equal can still be different. Men and women *are* different, and for the most part we process differently and come to buying decisions differently. Because of that, we cannot treat our male and female clients in identical ways. It is to your advantage to study gender differences to gain practical knowledge that will help you relate better to others based on their communication styles, and adapt your messages and marketing accordingly. Learn how to speak what I refer to as "MENglish® and WOMENglish®," and gain the authority, trust, reputation, influence, and market share you always dreamed of.

About Andrea Jones

If men are from Mars and women are from Venus, then Andrea Jones is definitely from Earth, providing a middle-ground perspective to men and women in both their personal and professional relationships with the other gender.

Andrea has more than twenty years of experience as a woman working in leadership positions in male-dominated environments. She was for example the one and only female business manager of a professional men's basketball team in Europe for over ten years.

Andrea is a certified personal coach, corporate trainer, and international speaker.

Learn More Here:
Menglish.com

Conclusion
by Kimberly Pitts

Upon hearing the word "influence," many people immediately think power, prestige, or a person of importance. While the word can mean that to some, the truth is that influence is directly tied to how you perceive your significance to those around you. To be an entrepreneur of influence, you have to truly see how significant and valuable your skills are to others. Before you can engage, before you market yourself, before you step out that front door, you must see the "influencer" in you. You must decide you are a person of influence.

When I entered this world of coaching and mentoring, I was aware that since my name was not well known, I would struggle with people trusting me. I will share with you that while I personally have never had a desire to be "known" for the sake of being known, I do care about being an influencer to those I coach and to those I am around each day.

I had to make a decision to be an influencer in my market. Then, I focused on creating meaningful engagement, and positioning myself in a way that those who liked my style would be drawn to work with me. Notice I said my style. You need to discover how to design a business brand that is reflective of who you are.

We have all seen people who claim they have knowledge, expertise, and know-how so they can get the sale or gain a new client. Your business branding can be hard if you are not truly operating in your areas of expertise. Bring your style and expertise to the surface. Make it genuine and believable.

This is what the overall purpose of this book was designed to do. My goal in compiling this work was to:

- Help you recognize new ways in which you can engage and communicate your value with your brand

- Provide you with new paradigm shifts into how you can create greater levels of engagement with your audience

- Equip and ignite in you a desire to revisit all that you are doing, and look for new ways to enhance your level of influence

It is my hope that we have accomplished this through the pages within this book, and that you are now on your way to becoming an influential entrepreneur, one who is positioned and *ready* for win-win engagement.

To Your Influence and Success!

Kimberly Pitts

www.ingramcontent.com/pod-product-compliance
Lightning Source LLC
LaVergne TN
LVHW022317060326
832902LV00020B/3520